HOLDING THE NET

Barnes & Noble Booksellers #1962
392 State Road Route 6
North Dartmouth, MA 02747
508-997-0701

STR:1962 REG:002 TRN:5355 CSHR:Nancy M

CUSTOMER ORDER PICKUP
ORDER NUMBER: 1962-275542

Holding the Net: Caring for My Mother on
9780998701226   T1
(1 @ 19.95)   19.95

Subtotal   19.95
Sales Tax T1 (6.250%)   1.25
TOTAL   21.20
VISA   21.20
  Card#: XXXXXXXXXXXX9273
  Expdate: XX/XX
  Auth: 011240
  Entry Method: Chip Read

  Application Label: VISA CREDIT
  AID: a0000000031010
  TVR: 8080008000
  TSI: 6800

A MEMBER WOULD HAVE SAVED   2.00

Connect with us on Social Media

Facebook- @BNNorthDartmouthMA
Instagram- @bn_dartmouth
Twitter- @BNDartmouth

055.01C   08/11/2021 06:54PM

CUSTOMER COPY

With a sales receipt or Barnes & Noble.com packing slip, a full refund in the original form of payment will be issued from any Barnes & Noble Booksellers store for returns of new and unread books, and unopened and undamaged music CDs, DVDs, vinyl records, electronics, toys/games and audio books made within 30 days of purchase from a Barnes & Noble Booksellers store or Barnes & Noble.com with the below exceptions:

Undamaged NOOKs purchased from any Barnes & Noble Booksellers store or from Barnes & Noble.com may be returned within 14 days when accompanied with a sales receipt or with a Barnes & Noble.com packing slip or may be exchanged within 30 days with a gift receipt.

A store credit for the purchase price will be issued (i) when a gift receipt is presented within 60 days of purchase, (ii) for all textbook returns and exchanges, or (iii) when the original tender is PayPal.

Items purchased as part of a Buy One Get One or Buy Two, Get Third Free offer are available for exchange only, unless all items purchased as part of the offer are returned, in which case such items are available for a refund (in 30 days). Exchanges of the item sold at no cost are available only for items of equal or lesser value than the original cost of such item.

Opened music CDs, DVDs, vinyl records, electronics, toys/games and audio books may not be returned, and can be exchanged only for the same product and only if defective. NOOKs purchased from other retailers or sellers are returnable only to the retailer or seller from which they were purchased pursuant to such retailer's or seller's return policy. Magazines, newspapers, eBooks, digital downloads, and used books are not returnable or exchangeable. Defective NOOKs may be exchanged at the store in accordance with the applicable warranty.

Returns or exchanges will not be permitted (i) after 30 days or without receipt or (ii) for product not carried by Barnes & Noble.com, (iii) for purchases made with a check less than 7 days prior to the date of return.

Policy on receipt may appear in two sections.

Return Policy

With a sales receipt or Barnes & Noble.com packing slip, a full refund in the original form of payment will be issued from any Barnes & Noble Booksellers store for returns of new and unread books, and unopened and undamaged music CDs, DVDs, vinyl records, electronics, toys/games and audio books made within 30 days of purchase from a Barnes & Noble Booksellers store or Barnes & Noble.com with the below exceptions:

Undamaged NOOKs purchased from any Barnes & Noble Booksellers store or from Barnes & Noble.com may be returned within 14 days

HOLDING THE NET

Caring for My Mother
on the Tightrope of Aging

MELANIE P. MERRIMAN

WITH A FOREWORD BY

Ann Hood

GREEN PLACE BOOKS | GREEN WRITERS PRESS

Brattleboro, Vermont

Printed in the United States

10 9 8 7 6 5 4 3 2 1

GREEN WRITERS PRESS is a Vermont-based publisher whose mission is to spread a message of hope and renewal through the words and images we publish. Throughout we will adhere to our commitment to preserving and protecting the natural resources of the earth. To that end, a percentage of our proceeds will be donated to environmental activist groups and a charity of the author's choice. Green Writers Press gratefully acknowledges support from individual donors, friends, and readers to help support the environment and our publishing initiative. GREEN PLACE BOOKS curates books that tell literary and compelling stories with a focus on writing about place—these books are more personal stories/memoir and biographies.

Giving Voice to Writers & Artists Who Will Make the World a Better Place
Green Writers Press | Brattleboro, Vermont
www.greenwriterspress.com

Library of Congress Cataloging-in-Publication Data available upon request.

ISBN: 978-0-9987012-2-6

COVER PHOTO: JÜTE@FLICKR.COM

THIS BOOK WAS PRINTED ON 30% PCR STOCK.
PRINTED BY THOMSON-SHORE.

Contents

Foreword

IN THE LAST ACT OF *Macbeth*, the main character makes reference to "…that which should accompany old age, as honour, love, obedience, troops of friends." Were truer words ever spoken? Honor, love, obedience, and troops of friends should accompany us into our old age—but how to accomplish that?

This was the goal Melanie Merriman and her sister Barbara had for their mother after their father died suddenly. At seventy-eight, Merriman's mother was still able to live independently in the condo that she and her husband had shared. Active in her community, she played bridge, participated in not one but two book clubs, and edited *The Comet*, her condo association's monthly newsletter. At that point, Merriman's hope of making "the rest of her [mother's] life the best it could possibly be" did not seem difficult.

Time marched on, however, and aging began to take its toll. One-third of people in the United States who are over sixty-five need some help in managing their daily lives; by the time they reach eighty-five (the fastest-growing segment of our population today), that number jumps to well over one-half.

Ten years after her husband died, Merriman's mother—then eighty-eight—began to voice her desire to never be dependent on her daughters. "I'm going to stay in my condo until I die," she told them two months before her eighty-ninth birthday. Yet friends were warning Merriman and her sister that their mother was slowing down, an idea they rejected at first. It's difficult to accept that a parent is no longer "aging well." My guess is that everyone reading this has faced a similar point in life, or watched a friend or family member deal with a parent (or both parents) as they struggle with independence, health issues, and emotional or mental decline.

According to the U.S. Census Bureau, America's population of persons aged ninety and older has tripled since 1980, reaching 1.9 million in 2010. Over the next forty years, that number will increase to 7.6 million. Wan He, the Census Bureau demographer, stated, "Traditionally, the cutoff age for what is considered the 'oldest old' has been 85, but people are living longer and the older population itself is getting older." And getting older means needing more care. More than 20% of people in their nineties live in nursing homes, and over 80% of people in their nineties have at least one disability.

Grace Paley wrote: "Old age is another country, a place of strangeness, sometimes, and dislocation." Melanie Merriman and her sister found themselves navigating that place of strangeness, which in today's world includes supportive living arrangements, the healthcare system, myriad professionals, and the person who is aging. In his poem "Affirmation," eighty-nine-year-old poet Donald Hall wrote, "To grow old is to lose everything." But Merriman—like adult children everywhere—vowed to make it otherwise for her mother. With honesty, nostalgia, humor, tenderness, and wisdom, she tells the story of their journey in *Holding the Net: Caring for My Mother on the Tightrope of Aging.*

Sixteen years after the phone call bringing the news that her father had died, Merriman's mother died at the age of ninety-four. This is the story of those years. It is the story of mothers and daughters. It is the story of aging in America today. It is the story of failures and successes in the decisions required to help someone age well. Most importantly, it is not the story of just one mother and her daughters.

It is all of our stories—ones already lived, or ones midstream, or ones about to happen. Read Melanie Merriman's words for validation, for forgiveness, for guidance, for hope. The tightrope of aging contains all of these, and more. This book will hold your hand on that tightrope.

Ann Hood
MAY, 2017

Preface

WHEN MY EIGHTY-YEAR-OLD FATHER died suddenly, my mother dealt with her grief by keeping busy. She joined a second book club, played more bridge, and intensified her community activities. Though it was hard to imagine her slowing down, I knew things would change as she aged. With my father gone, I appointed myself to look after Mom. I wanted to make the rest of her life the best it could possibly be.

I reasonably expected that this wouldn't be too difficult. First, my mother had the resources to pay for whatever care she might need. Second, I worked in the field of hospice and palliative care, so I knew more than most people do about illness, aging, and our overly complex medical system. Third, I had a supportive sibling: my sister, Barbara.

It turned out that my rational expectations could not have been more wrong. Despite my many distinct advantages, caring for my mother as she declined both physically and mentally proved humbling. Emotions overwhelmed reason, and my professional knowledge paled next to my lack of real-world experience. My sister Barbara and I desperately wanted to do the right things for our mother, but we were never sure what the right things were. Every decision pitted Mom's desire for independence against our fear for her safety on what I came to think of as the tightrope of aging.

After Mom died, I looked up from my head-down focus on her immediate needs and realized that most of my friends—and even strangers I talked to in line at the grocery store or coffee shop—were living through some version of this tightrope walk with aging parents. I also found that in sharing our stories, we were giving each other something we desperately needed: validation that caring for a parent is unwelcome and unfamiliar for all concerned.

I wrote *Holding the Net* to help as many people in this situation as possible. People with aging parents who want to know what to expect. People who cared for an elderly parent who died, and wonder whether they did it well. Even aging parents themselves, who want, as my mother so desperately wanted, not to be a burden to their children.

I cannot offer a foolproof recipe for helping a parent age with grace. In my experience, the ingredients are too human, and the healthcare system is too flawed. But when children willingly offer support—and when, even more rarely, parents willingly accept that support—there can be moments that feel perfect. That is where grace comes in.

To help you find more of those perfect moments, and better deal with the difficult ones, I have laid bare both my successes and my failures in caring for my mother. I have shared what I knew going in—or discovered along the way—about supportive living arrangements, healthcare services, medical decision-making, professionals you can turn to for help, and more. While I don't have all the answers, you can learn from my experience, and may feel comforted to see that uncertainty and confusion are normal when caring for an aging parent.

Everything in this book is true, and told as I remember it. While some of the dialogue is improvised, all of it is based upon actual conversations or written communication. The people and places exist, and for most of them, I have used real names. In cases for which I wanted to protect an identity, names have been changed.

There are three people without whom this book would never have come to be: Andrea Askowitz, who provided encouragement on the first day of my first writing class, and made me believe I could be a writer; my sister, Barbara, who helped with research, provided insightful feedback on multiple versions of the text, and often guided me to the truth; and my husband, Klein, whose love and support are the warp and weft of my personal safety net.

HOLDING THE NET

Chapter 1

THREE WEEKS BEFORE HIS EIGHTY-FIRST BIRTHDAY, my father died only moments after complimenting my mother on dinner—lamb chops, mashed potatoes, and asparagus. When my phone rang on that night of February 28, 1994, I was in Miami, some three hundred miles away, entertaining friends in the house I shared with my fiancé, Klein.

"Daddy's gone," Mom said as soon as I picked up the phone. I held the receiver in one hand and grabbed the kitchen doorknob with the other as I slid down the wall to the floor.

"What happened?" I asked.

"I don't know. I was going to the kitchen to fix coffee after we ate, and I heard him cough and choke a little. Then he just stopped. I didn't hear anything but the TV."

"Was it a heart attack?" I asked.

"A stroke, I think. I went back to check on him, and his head was down. I grabbed his shoulders, and he was just limp. So I called 911. It happened so fast!"

"Mom, are you okay?" I was thinking about how and when I could get across the state to New Port Richey to be with her.

"I'm here with the rescue squad. They'll stay with me until the funeral home comes. And Ginny is coming down. I think she'll stay overnight if I want her to."

Ginny, their second-floor neighbor, was a widow with a big extended Italian family that included good friends like my parents. I knew she would take good care of Mom.

"Oh, Mom, I'm never going to see him again, am I?" I was crying.

"No, honey."

I knew exactly where the paramedics had found him—slumped in his chair in the sunroom of the condo. Every evening, my parents sat in the matching rattan chairs, on cushions decorated with brushstrokes of pale blue, violet, and pink. They watched the news, and maybe a documentary on PBS, while enjoying a dry martini and dinner served on teak TV tables. In the mornings, they drank coffee poured from a thermal carafe at the rattan table by the glass sliding doors, ate fruit and toast, and worked on the daily crossword puzzle while watching the occasional boat glide down the canal, just a few steps away.

"Kiss him for me. Please, Mom, kiss him on his cheek."

"Okay, honey, I will." My mother sounded overly calm, but then again, we were a pragmatic family. Faced with a problem, we got right to solutions, and tried to return to normal as quickly as possible.

"Mom, I think it's too late for me to get a plane into Tampa tonight. Did you talk to Barbara?"

Barbara, four years older and my only sibling, lived in Arlington, Virginia, just a few miles from where we grew up.

"I'm going to call her now," Mom said.

"Do you want me to call her?" I asked.

"No, I'll do it."

"Tell her to call me so we can coordinate our flights. We'll hook up at the Tampa airport tomorrow and rent a car." Now I was in problem-solving mode.

"I can pick you up."

"No, Mom, let us get a car. I'll call you in the morning. If you need anything, though, call me tonight. Call me anytime. I'll keep the phone by the bed. I love you, Mom."

In our small family circus, Daddy had played the role of benevolent owner. He had supported us all through his hard work and smart investment decisions. He'd kept the tent mended, and entertained us with bad jokes and painfully clever puns. Mom was the ringmaster, making sure the show ran smoothly. She encouraged my desire to perform, and tried to coax Barbara from her chosen seat behind the curtain. Barbara and I were expected to be responsible and proceed with caution, but Mom and Daddy always offered a safety net if we got into trouble.

In recent weeks, Daddy had been the one in trouble.

"He keeps saying he just doesn't feel like himself," Mom had told me a few days earlier.

They'd seen the doctor that morning, and Daddy was scheduled for tests the following Monday to see if his carotid artery, the one that carries oxygenated blood to the brain, was partially blocked.

I'd been worried for a while. A month before Daddy died, I'd called to tell my parents the good news that Klein and I were engaged. I was forty-two and this was my second marriage, the first having ended ten years before in an unpleasant divorce. Mom and Daddy had met Klein. They liked him, and could see that we were happy together.

Daddy answered the call, and I told him how Klein had proposed on Valentine's Day on the beach. He said, "That's good, Mel, real good. Mom's not here, but I'll tell her as soon as she comes back." His voice was flat, and it scared me. The man I grew up with would have whooped and said something like, "Geez, Mel, that's the nuts! He is one lucky guy." I hung up the phone and cried. I knew Daddy had suffered a few small strokes, but until that conversation, I hadn't realized how much they were robbing him of his ability to feel or express his usual *joie de vivre*.

The day after Daddy's death, Barbara and I met at the Avis counter at the Tampa airport. Her eyes were red, and we both teared up when we hugged. On the forty-five-minute drive to Gulf Harbors, we caught up on our lives and work, laughed about Daddy's favorite landmark—the giant white, red, and green concrete cowboy boots at the entrance to Boot Ranch, home of Al Boyd's award-winning Brahman cattle—and speculated about what had killed our father.

Had a stroke brought on the choking, or the other way around? Did it matter?

At the condo, we dragged our suitcases into the narrow front hallway and called to Mom. Everything seemed the same as always—the immaculate lettuce-green carpet, the dim light filtering in from the sunroom, the small arrangement of blue and white silk flowers on the dining table, the quiet hum of the air conditioning, and the faintly sweet, leathery smell of Daddy's pipe tobacco. Was he really gone?

Mom came out of the bedroom. Even she looked unchanged—sturdy, well-groomed, and, at five-foot-one and one hundred-forty pounds, nicely cushioned. Her thin white hair was teased into a poufy cloud above light blue eyes, a large, straight nose, and bright red lips. She wore her uniform of indestructible polyester knit stretch slacks, print blouse, and suede-strapped wedge sandals. Barbara and I moved in for a group hug, creating a five-foot pillar of Pratt women.

"I'm okay, really, I'm okay," Mom said. "Put your suitcases in the guest room, and let's have some lunch."

We each made a sandwich from the cold cuts Mom had laid out, and took them to the table in the sunroom.

"What happens next?" I asked Mom.

As usual, she was ready to face the situation head-on and take charge. Mom was smart—Swarthmore, class of 1937 smart—and supremely capable. Before Barbara was born, Mom had worked as an editor at the John C. Winston Company, then as assistant to the medical director at Capital Airlines. When Barbara and I were growing up, Mom had run our home like a skilled executive from her turquoise Formica-topped desk in the kitchen. She'd kept track of our school activities, doctor's appointments, ballet and piano lessons, and Daddy's work shifts as a maintenance dispatcher (also at Capital Airlines). Everything was marked on the Girl Scout calendar that sat below the yellow wall phone with the long, coiled cord. Next to the calendar was the flip-up A-to-Z aluminum telephone directory, with numbers for doctors, schools, the housekeeper, and all our friends, available at the touch of a button.

Mom still had that ancient directory, with old entries crossed out and newer ones in various colors of ink. She'd been using it all morning.

"We'll have to go to the funeral home tomorrow and finalize everything. You know he'll be cremated. I called Keith at Merrill Lynch, and the lawyer, and the accountant. We can't do anything else until I get the death certificate," Mom said.

Barbara and I knew all about our parents' finances. On more than one of my previous visits, Daddy had sat me down at the breakfast table and pulled out the three-ring binder of Merrill Lynch statements. He'd explained over and over how all their assets were in a living trust that would make it easy to transfer everything to Mom, or to him if she died first, and to me and Barb, once they were both gone. He had made sure Barbara and I could locate the keys to the fireproof safe that sat on the floor of the storage closet. In it were the trust documents, wills, living wills, and paperwork for their prepaid cremation.

Next to the safe was the file cabinet with medical records, insurance documents, utility bills, and condo papers. Daddy and Mom each had a file labeled *In Case of Death*—as if it were optional.

After lunch, I went into the closet, pulled out Daddy's folder, and read through the contents: a copy of the prose poem *Desiderata*, by Max Ehrmann; a list, written on a piece of lined yellow legal paper, of some of his favorite music, including *The Planets* by Gustav Holst and Carl Orff's cantata, *Carmina Burana*; a letter from someone he had worked with at Capital Airlines, praising his sound judgment and sense of fairness; and an autobiography in Daddy's handwriting from his junior year of high school. He'd received an A+. I had never seen them before, but each item reflected how deeply he had cared about people, and the way he had wanted to be remembered.

I have to write a eulogy, I thought. *We have to have a service.* Daddy's death had been too sudden. I wanted to keep him alive a little longer. I wanted to honor his memory, and give others the chance to honor him, as well.

I told Barbara my idea.

"Look, I'd really like to do something, too, but you know Mom won't want to," she said.

Mom and Daddy had said many times that they did not want any kind of funeral service. I'll never know why they felt so strongly. Maybe they thought funerals were sad, and even if they couldn't protect us from death, they would try to protect us from sadness. After they had mentioned it two or three times, I probed a little to see what might be acceptable.

"Can't we at least invite people over for brunch?" I'd asked them. "Your friends will want to pay their respects."

"We just don't want any fuss," Mom said.

"There's no need to make a big deal," Daddy added.

At five o' clock, Barbara, Mom, and I headed to the sunroom with our drinks. Mom sat in her chair, and Barbara and I sat in the side chairs that rocked and swiveled. No one sat in Daddy's chair.

I leaned over to the TV table holding the snacks, dipping some hummus onto a cracker.

"Mom, I want to have a service for Daddy."-

"Mel, you know he didn't want anything like that," Mom replied.

"I know he said he didn't, but then he carefully prepared all this." I picked up the blue folder.

"We both have folders," Mom said. "It's stuff to use in an obituary."

I rocked my chair a couple of times.

"Mom, I just think there is a lot more to say than what we can put into an obituary. I want to tell people what he meant to me."

"I do, too," said Barbara, her voice catching.

Mom sipped her martini and reached for a tissue.

"I just don't know," she said, wiping her nose. "We always said, no services for us."

"Well, the service isn't *for* him, it's *about* him," I told her. "It's for me and you and Barbara, and for everyone else who wants to say goodbye. It doesn't have to be anything elaborate. Mom, I need to do this."

"Where would we have it? I can't do anything here." Mom looked down, folding her hands onto her lap. "And when would we have it? You girls need to get home, back to your lives and your jobs."

Barbara rattled the ice cubes in her bourbon. "Mom, we can stay for a few days. I can't even think about work right now, and Phil will be fine without me."

Barbara's first marriage, like mine, had ended in divorce. She had married her second husband, Phil, just three months before Daddy died. She didn't have children, but Phil had a son who spent some weekdays and weekends with them. Barbara worked as a paralegal, mostly on environmental cases and mass torts—like seeking compensation for families of holocaust survivors whose assets had been taken during the war—for a large firm in Washington, D.C.

Klein and I had no immediate plans for a wedding, and no children. My first career had been as a research scientist on the faculty at the University of Miami School of Medicine. In 1992, two years before Daddy died, I'd finished an MBA in Health Care Administration, and changed careers. Now I worked for a national provider of hospice services, home-based care for people near the end of life. They had a generous policy about bereavement leave.

"I agree," I said. "This is the only place I want to be right now."

"Well, I'm glad you're here," Mom said, "but you know Daddy wouldn't want any commotion."

"I know, but we don't have to pretend that nothing has happened," Barbara said. She picked up her glass and headed for the kitchen. "I need a refill."

"Look, Barbara and I will take care of all the arrangements," I said to Mom. "What about having it in one of the condo clubhouses?"

"No, you can't use the clubhouse for anything personal," Mom said.

"Maybe the funeral home would provide a room."

"Maybe." Mom spread some cheese on a cracker. I reached for the hummus and forced myself to keep quiet.

"Okay," said Mom, "but it won't be a funeral. It will be a memorial service."

"Good," I said. "A memorial service is just right. We can put the information about it into his obituary."

The next day at the funeral home, Mom signed all the papers for the cremation, and we asked if they would rent us a room where we could conduct a memorial service. The only room available was a chapel that held two hundred, far bigger than we needed. Mom thought it was expensive. As she took out her checkbook, I told her I would pay. She wouldn't let me, but said Barbara and I could buy some flowers to decorate the room.

Two days later, we were back at the funeral home, setting up for the service. The newspaper had made a mistake, and Daddy's obituary hadn't been printed yet, so we only expected a small group of his and Mom's closest friends.

Barbara placed the flowers at the front of the room, and I put a copy of *The Planets* on the CD player at low volume. Daddy had been a hi-fi buff, and I imagined him cringing at the pathetic sound system. Every night, when we were kids, he would go to the basement after dinner and listen to classical records or reel-to-reel tape recordings through two speakers the size of small refrigerators. After the move to the condo, he had to substitute smaller speakers, but they were still powerful.

"Sometimes, when your mom is out at the grocery store," he had once confessed to me, "I crank up the volume until the sheer beauty of the music shoves me up against the back wall, gasping for air."

At the service, Mom sat in the front row. She kept turning around to watch as more and more people arrived. Somehow, even without the obituary, word had spread about the memorial service. I thought about the ending of *It's a Wonderful Life*, and hoped that Daddy, like the Jimmy Stewart character in the movie, could see how much he had mattered.

My parents, Eleanor and Dave Pratt to their friends, were part of the fabric of their Gulf Harbors condominium community. They had moved in twenty years earlier, during one of the first phases of construction. Daddy considered a warm Florida retirement to be the reward for working hard and taking good care of his family. He'd had to drag Mom out of our Northern Virginia home, but within a year or so, she had settled in. She served as president of the 537-unit condo association for two years, then became editor of *The Comet,* the community newsletter. Daddy had a rack in a kitchen cupboard that held about ten sets of extra keys, each neatly labeled with the name of a couple who had asked him to check on their homes when they were out of town. Once, one of the clubhouses burned down, and Daddy had designed and overseen construction of the new one.

At the service, I read my eulogy, quoting Erhmann's *Desiderata* ("As far as possible, without surrender, be on good terms with all persons") and extolling Daddy's sense of personal responsibility and willingness to help anyone who needed it. "Whenever I see that bumper sticker about random acts of kindness and senseless acts of beauty," I said, "I always think of my dad."

Barbara shared what she called her "mental videos" of Daddy: when he taught her to drive while explaining the workings of the internal combustion engine; when he described why one should always tell the truth (because it's too hard to remember your lies); and when he was just enjoying life…the way he would lean back after a good meal with family and friends, put his hands on the table, roll his eyes to the heavens, and shout, "Man! I just love these kinds of carryings-on."

Though she had sworn she would not, Mom said a few words, then invited others to share memories. I don't think anyone said anything sad, other than the obvious—that he would be missed.

After the service, when everyone had left and we'd come back to the condo, Mom gave her assessment. "Okay," she said. "You can do a service like that for me."

I laughed and enjoyed a moment of self-satisfaction. "We'll see," I said. "It will be a long time before it's your turn."

And then it hit me. Mom was only seventy-eight, and had years ahead of her without Daddy.

I hadn't planned for this. I had spun myself a myth that my parents would go about their independent, happy lives—then, one day, they would die simultaneously, preferably in their sleep.

Until Daddy's recent strokes, they had been pretty much living my myth. They'd been married for fifty-three years, were still in love, and fulfilled comfortable, well-established roles. Mom did the grocery shopping, cooked the meals, and managed their social life. Daddy took care of the car, did minor maintenance projects in their condo, and managed the finances. They both cleaned the house and did laundry. Mom also kept busy with bridge and women's groups, her "job" as editor of *The Comet*, and arranging trips to dinner and the theater for condo residents. Daddy preferred to stay home and read or listen to music. He liked his routines, but he encouraged Mom to go and do whatever she enjoyed. And when she felt overwhelmed, he offered a warm hug and a calm voice to let her know it would all work out fine.

There had been only two hospitalizations, neither of crisis proportions. When she was seventy, Mom had been diagnosed with breast cancer. It was a tiny tumor, but at the time, standard treatment was a full mastectomy. There were no complications, and she didn't receive radiation or chemotherapy. The summer before he died, Daddy had back surgery, a routine laminectomy, to relieve pain in his leg.

In my hospice work, I was immersed in end-of-life scenarios that featured advanced illness and the need for intensive symptom management. I was becoming an expert in quality of life for hospice patients—but none of that would help me now. Daddy hadn't needed hospice care; he died almost before anyone realized he might be near the end of life. And Mom was very much alive and healthy.

My myth had been shattered.

The sunroom at Mom and Daddy's condo in New Port Richey, Florida. I took this picture in 2007.

Chapter 2

THE NIGHT OF THE MEMORIAL, Barbara and I, each with an opened book, tucked into the well-worn flowered sheets on the twin beds in Mom's guest room. After a few minutes, I realized I was reading the same paragraph over and over.

"How do you think Mom is doing?" I asked.

"She seems fine." Barbara kept reading.

"I know. Is that weird? Do you think she's in shock? Maybe I'll suggest she come home with me for a few days."

"She won't go. She doesn't want to…be a burden." We said those last three words together, like a chorus, and laughed.

This was Mom's frequent refrain, and though her motives were noble, it often came up in ways that seemed self-serving—like Daddy's 70th birthday dinner at Rossi's Italian Restaurant. We were playing *What if you won the lottery?* and Barbara had said she would quit her job and buy a big house with a greenhouse and lots of gardens. Her husband said he'd buy a Maserati. Daddy said "Me, too." Then it was Mom's turn.

"I just don't ever want to be a burden on my girls," she said.

We all blew her raspberries.

"No fair!" I said.

"No fun," said Barbara.

"Well, that's my answer," Mom had said as she wiped at her eyes with her napkin.

Game over.

I half sat up and leaned on my elbow to face Barbara in the other bed.

"But seriously," I said. "What happens now?"

After a moment, Barbara put down her book and looked straight ahead.

"I don't know," she said. "I just don't know."

If nothing else, I figured we would need to be there for Mom in ways that had simply been unnecessary before, and I knew it would be more me than Barbara. Of course, it was easier for me to visit from Miami than for Barbara to come down from Virginia—but the main reason it would be me was that Mom and I liked each other. Mom always said that she and I were *sympatico*. Barb and Mom, on the other hand, maintained a polite and superficial relationship. They rarely saw each other, and never spent more than a long weekend together. Mom and Barb were family. Mom and I were friends.

Mom and I had always been close. When I was young, I needed her, and she liked to be needed. I was eager to start school, so Mom put me in kindergarten at only four years old. Though intellectually more than ready, I was emotionally crippled by separation anxiety. Mom volunteered as a teacher's assistant so she could be in the classroom for the first few hours of each day until I got my sea legs. I didn't understand exactly what was going on, but even then, I knew I would not have made it without her.

Also, Mom and I were both extroverts who liked to go and see and do. Mom had to push Barbara to join the Brownies, while I begged to be in their talent show two years before I was old enough to join the troop. Like Mom, who had been in plays in high school, I was eager to take ballet and be in the recitals, in spite of terrible stage fright. Mom encouraged all my exploits.

Even through my senior year in high school, I'd come home from school and tell Mom all about my day. She was interested. She offered advice. We didn't always agree, but we always wanted to know what the other thought.

Barbara was more of an introvert, and she liked her privacy. When she came home from school, she headed straight for her room and shut the door. Mom was just as eager to hear about Barbara's day, and just as eager to share her opinions about what Barbara should do—but Barbara didn't seem to care what Mom thought, or what Mom wanted her to do. Like most teenagers, she cared more about what her friends thought.

Mom had strong opinions, which she stated as if they were fact. Instead of saying "I like your hair better short," she'd say, "Your hair looks better short."

I ignored it, but Barbara bristled.

"I like it long," Barbara would say.

Mom tried other ways to connect, pressing Barb for information.

"How are things at school? Did you decide to write for the newspaper?" Mom might ask when Barbara came into the kitchen for a snack.

"School's okay. I haven't decided about the paper." Barbara would stare into the open refrigerator. Then she'd grab an apple, take a bite, and head back down the hall to her room.

I loved Barbara. I wanted to be her. I couldn't wait to fit into her hand-me-downs—but I didn't feel like I mattered much to her. And really, why would she want to be my friend? She was four years older, and I was a fragile, nerdy, goody-two-shoes. Knowing that my frequent attacks of nerves disrupted the family, I tried to compensate by bringing home excellent grades, staying out of trouble, and doing whatever was asked of me. For the most part, Barbara and I were just two people growing up in the same house.

As we got older, graduated college, and married our first husbands—and as I became more independent, less fragile emotionally, and less attached to Mom—Barbara and I started building a real friendship. Then we discovered we had a lot more in common than we'd ever thought. The anxiety I'd suffered as a little girl continued into adulthood in the form of panic attacks. I'd have good months and bad months, even good years and bad years. I knew something was wrong with me. I didn't want anyone else to know. I lived a full life, but cautiously.

When I was twenty-four and Barbara was twenty-eight, she had her first panic attack, and then another and another, until the unpredictability and severity of the symptoms developed into agoraphobia. She was afraid to go anywhere or do anything. She thought she was going crazy. Finally, knowing I would understand because of my own struggles, she called me.

"You are not crazy," I told her. "I know it feels that way, but I promise, you can and will get better. I'll send you the name of the psychiatrist I used to see. He's good. He'll help you."

"Could you call him for me?" She was crying so hard I could barely understand her.

"Yes," I said, "I'll get the first available appointment. Will Skip take you?" Skip was Barbara's first husband.

"I don't want to ask him. He's been completely supportive, but I'm afraid he'll get tired of my being so dependent on him."

"Do you want me to come down?" I asked.

I was in the last stages of my PhD program at Brandeis University in Waltham, MA, deep into editing my thesis.

"Oh, Melly!" I heard fresh tears. "How can you do that? I wish you could."

"I can, and I will," I said. "I'll be there tomorrow."

I threw my thesis and some clothes into a suitcase and flew to Virginia. I found Barbara curled up on the couch in her living room, wrapped in a blanket. As we hugged, she sobbed into my shoulder. Years later, she would tell me that she had been afraid and anxious as a kid, just as I was; that she'd been furious with Mom for making her do things she was afraid of, like joining clubs and performing. Her bedroom was her escape, the safe place where she could retreat from the real world into a book. But this full-on, uncontrollable panic was new to her.

"I promise this will get better," I told her. "I have been there, and I know there are ways out."

"I hate this. I hate myself. Why can't I get up and fight?" she asked.

"It's biochemistry," I explained, "not a moral failing. You're all out of whack. I don't know why, but I know it's not your fault. We have an appointment with the doctor tomorrow morning. That's the first step."

I stayed for a week, and when I left, Barbara was still shaky, but able to go to work. Over the next few months, with the help of medication and counseling, she returned to her new normal—mostly her old self, but living more cautiously, just like me.

After that, we continued to grow closer every year. We traveled to Europe together. She helped me move out when I left my first husband. We visited each other for fun.

I guess Mom could see it. She started nagging me about Barbara.

"She talks to you, doesn't she? Do you think she's happy?"

Leave her alone, I wanted to say.

In my experience, people don't change significantly over time. Once you get to know them, you decide whether you want to accept them as they are, be friends, and spend time together—or not. I'm rarely disappointed in my friends, because I don't expect them to be any different than they are.

Mom wanted Barbara to be different than she was. Mom wanted Barbara to be more open about her life. She wanted Barbara to be more like her. And Barbara, rightfully, resented it. She knew Mom loved her, but she wanted Mom to accept her just as she was. And the more that didn't happen, the more Barbara kept her distance.

With Daddy gone, I was the one who would be there for Mom. She had always been my biggest supporter. All I wanted now was to be *her* biggest supporter. I would do whatever I could to help her have the best life possible without Daddy. I had no idea what that might mean, for her or for me.

Chapter 3

WHEN I WAS LITTLE, one of my favorite books was *Helpful Henry*, about a little boy who tries to help around the house, often with disastrous results. It became a family joke, because Mom often mistakenly referred to the book as "Helpless Henry," but it wasn't a joke to me. I always aspired to be the helpful one. In the first year after Daddy died, I remembered Henry, and took my vow to be Mom's biggest supporter very seriously.

Mom was seventy-eight when Daddy died, but she looked and acted much younger. She kept busy with her friends, most of whom actually were younger. She had something penciled in for every day on the calendar she kept on the kitchen counter: bridge, hairdresser, book club, luncheons with her university women's group. I knew she had a lot of support from her friends, and that her days would be happily occupied. I cringed, though, at the thought of her sitting in that sunroom eating dinner on one of the teak TV trays alone.

I called every few days. She filled me in on the details of modifying the living trust, transferring the car title, and generally setting herself up as sole owner and manager of her life. If she said she was feeling down, I'd offer to visit.

She always refused. "You have your work and your life. And you'd only be here a few days. I'll be alright. I'm just a little sad today."

I made sure she had company on all the major holidays. Barbara and I went to New Port Richey for Mother's Day, and made brunch for Mom and her friend Lenore.

Mom and Daddy knew lots of people at Gulf Harbors, but it wasn't until Lenore moved into one of the condos that Mom found someone who felt like a sister. Lenore, like Mom, was a college graduate. They both loved books and plays and concerts. Lenore had traveled and lived overseas, something Mom had always wanted to do. They liked to talk about ideas, opinions, and feelings. Lenore was a widow, and when Daddy died, she and Mom had one more thing in common.

On Father's Day, Mom sent Barb and me framed reprints of a picture of Daddy at the beach with his two little girls. I cried at the thoughtfulness and pure sentimentality.

In August, Klein and I got married in Hawaii during a family vacation with all of Klein's family. Two weeks before we left for the trip to the islands, I had talked to Mom on the phone.

"Why don't you get married when you're there?" she'd suggested.

"Well, we could, but I know you wouldn't come, and I don't think Barbara could come, either," I countered.

"I don't mind," she said. "I was at your first wedding. It's okay if I miss this one."

"Really?" I was surprised, but kind of relieved. A Hawaiian beach sounded like the perfect place for a wedding to me.

"Really. I didn't go to Barbara's second wedding, either."

She was right. While I felt like I had married into Klein's larger family—and happily so—he hadn't had many opportunities to bond with my tiny one. For that matter, neither had Barbara's second husband, Phil.

Though Klein and Phil never really got close to Mom, Barbara and I continued to bring the family together now and then. In November, we were all at Barbara's house in Arlington for Thanksgiving. Barbara and I had decided to try brining the turkey. We were looking in the garage for an ice chest large enough to hold the turkey and the cold brining mixture.

"Do you have to do that? It seems like a lot of trouble," Mom said.

"Ugh, can't she stay out of it?" Barbara hissed to me. "Nobody's asking her to cook the bird."

"That's just how she is," I said, chuckling. "Remember that time at Bern's?"

"Oh, my God," Barbara laughed. "That was too much!"

Bern's Steak House, a world-famous restaurant known for its telephone-book-sized wine list, had been Daddy's favorite place for celebratory meals. He and Mom latched onto specific waiters—first it was the young, blond Dean, and when he left, they had adopted Jamal. We had previously toured the wine cellar, and on this particular occasion, Mom asked for a kitchen tour, because she, Barbara, and I all enjoyed cooking so much.

When we finished our meal, we headed into the kitchen with one of the assistant managers. The heat, the noise, and the sense of organized chaos amazed me. I wanted to linger, but I kept up with the group. As we all exited the kitchen, we realized we'd lost Mom. We waited a minute, then two, then three. Finally, the manager went in to find her.

"What happened?" I asked Mom when she emerged.

"I stopped to talk to the guy sautéing the carrots. I told him he was using too much almond flavoring," Mom replied.

"Mo-om," Barbara and I moaned in unison.

"What? I thought he'd want to know. I would."

That was Mom—sure she knew best. I accepted it. Barbara got annoyed. Klein and Phil found it irritating, and felt defensive when Barbara or I were on the receiving end of Mom's "corrections."

A month after Thanksgiving, Mom visited Klein and me in Miami for Christmas.

I decorated the tree before she arrived, even though this violated the family tradition. When we were kids, the Christmas tree had always gone up in the corner of the living room on December 24th and stayed up until Epiphany on Jan 6th. Instead of putting presents under the tree, Daddy would set out the elaborate foldable green platform he had built for his model train set. Each year, Barbara and

I set out the village of miniature houses Daddy had put together from kits, along with tiny rubber trees, fake snow, and a compact mirror for a skating pond. We delighted in placing the little plastic guy, who looked like he was running with a lantern, just a few steps short of the outhouse.

"Your tree looks lovely," Mom said now. "I have some decorations in the condo, but I'll never put up a tree again. It reminds me too much of your dad."

I thought about all the things that reminded me of Daddy: classical music, bad puns, and the smell of pipe tobacco. He was the reason I shook the bottle to get out every bit of the catsup, and rolled up the toothpaste tube to get the last squirt. He had always quoted the Great Depression adage: "Use it up, wear it out, make it do, or do without."

By Easter of 1995, Daddy had been gone for a year. Mom's life settled into a comfortable routine that featured her friends, bridge luncheons, her role as historian of the local chapter of the American Association of University Women, her book club, and, most importantly, editing the condo's monthly newsletter.

Mom had taken over *The Comet* in 1977, just a few years after moving to Gulf Harbors, though "taken over" seems too mild a description. It became her mission, her vocation, her welcome daily touchstone.

She was proud of how she'd redesigned the masthead by tracing a picture of a real comet, and using letter stencils from the art store to give the title some character. She'd also added an "editorial" on page one.

"I aim for timely, but never controversial," she said. "I always keep it light."

In January, her topic usually included one or two New Year's resolutions. In the spring, she might write about Peter Rabbit, including a brief bio of his creator, Beatrix Potter. In October, she held forth on Halloween myths.

For eighteen years, she had compiled *The Comet* every month, and managed its distribution to over five hundred residents. At first, she had typed it on a stencil, and Daddy had helped run off copies on a mimeograph machine. Then Xerox copiers came along, and she typed the master on plain paper before taking it to the office supply store for copying. In the mid-1980s, Mom learned to use a computer, and typed *The Comet* using WordPerfect. When the office at Gulf Harbors purchased new computers, Mom had to learn how to use Microsoft Word.

"That damned mouse is impossible," she told me.

At seventy-nine, she was still going to the condo office every morning to work on *The Comet* for a few hours. She would never visit me the last week of the month, because that's when the newsletter was printed and distributed.

In the years following Daddy's death, I continued my hospice work, eventually leaving my job at the hospice company and working from home as an independent consultant. In collaboration with two physician colleagues, Ira Byock and Barry Kinzbrunner, I developed and published an index to assess quality of life for people nearing the end of life. I also gained a modest reputation for my work in the development and implementation of other measures of hospice quality, such as pain management and patient/family satisfaction with care. I traveled often to help hospices across the country improve their quality, work with colleagues on quality measure development, and train hospice staff in the use of the quality of life index.

Mom was well-known to anyone who heard me speak on improving quality and best practices. I used her chocolate chip cookies as an example of how we all think we know (and are practicing) the optimal way to do our jobs, but sometimes, we don't know what we don't know. I explained that she made the best chocolate chip cookies on the planet, and she told me she used the recipe on the package of Nestlé Toll House Morsels. I used the same recipe, and my cookies were never as good as hers, so one day, I insisted we make them together. It turned out that she used margarine instead of Crisco, mixed with a wooden spoon instead of an electric mixer, and baked the cookies at a slightly lower temperature than the recipe called for. We were both following the recipe; we were just following it differently. This story always hit home for nurses who worked alone in the field, one-on-one with patients, and it stimulated lots of discussion about how to discover and share best practices.

One hospice I worked with was near Tampa, only a few miles from New Port Richey, so I had opportunities to visit Mom every few months. I typically spent the day lecturing about quality of life at the end of life, then drove down Highway 19 to spend the night with Mom at her condo. I arrived right at cocktail time.

My drink was a Jim Beam Manhattan with a cherry. Mom's was a Tanqueray martini, on the rocks, very dry, with an olive or two. She considered the switch from Gordon's, Daddy's gin, to Tanqueray an extravagance.

"I always remind myself how lucky I am to be able to afford it," she told me.

"I think Daddy would approve," I replied.

Mom usually put out some cheese and crackers, and we would sit side by side in the matching rattan chairs in the sunroom. Mom sat in Daddy's chair, and I sat in hers.

By this time, she was in her early eighties and I was in my late forties, but we'd gab like girlfriends.

"My book club is reading *Memoirs of a Geisha*," Mom said. "Some parts are really brutal, but it's a good book. You would love it."

"Will you send it to me when you're done?"

"Sure, sure."

"I'm so disappointed in Bill Clinton. Why didn't he just tell the truth about Monica Lewinsky?" I asked.

"I know. Better to be a sex fiend than a liar, I always say," Mom replied.

Often, I would peruse the most recent issue of *The Comet* as Mom told me her ideas for her next editorial. I told her about my business trips.

"You work too hard," she said. "I swear, they're going to bury you with that computer."

She almost always reminded me about her memorial service.

"Be sure to turn the music up. People at Daddy's service said they couldn't hear it."

"Mom, your service is a long way away. You've barely even slowed down. You're acting like the White Queen, crying out before anything bad has happened," I said.

"Well, I am slowing down. You just don't see it. And even if it is far away, once it happens, I won't be there to remind you."

I assured her I would turn the music up as loud as possible.

Then she would serve a home-cooked dinner on the teak TV trays, and together, we would solve the *Wheel of Fortune* puzzles. We were both smarter than any of the contestants.

Four years after Daddy died, shortly after Mom turned eighty-two, we had a scare. She slipped when getting down from the examination table at her doctor's office and broke her wrist. By the time she called me, she was at home with her right arm—her dominant arm—in a cast that went past her elbow.

"I'll come right away," I said, "I have a meeting tomorrow morning, but I can miss it."

Her voice was shaky, but she assured me she would be fine until I could get there the next afternoon.

"I'm not feeling too bad right now." Lenore, her best friend, had picked her up at the hospital and taken her to get the prescription filled for her pain medication.

"But Mom, how will you get ready for bed and everything?"

"Ginny's on her way now to help me."

I gave silent thanks for Ginny, Mom's dependable upstairs neighbor and close friend.

"Call me if you need anything—or have Ginny call me," I said.

"Try not to worry," Mom said. "I'll see you tomorrow."

When I arrived the next day, I found Mom alone, sitting at the table in the silent, darkening sunroom, propping her cast up with her left hand. On the table next to her sat a half a glass of water and the cordless phone. She barely looked up as I called to her.

"Mel," she sobbed, "I can barely move. What am I going to do?"

I put my arms around her and rocked her, stifling my own tears of shame for not coming sooner.

"It'll be alright," I said, "I'm going to take of care of you."

It broke my heart to see her suffer. I found the information from the hospital and checked her prescription bottle. I gave her two pills and made her eat some sliced apple, cheese, and crackers. For the first time ever, I helped her use the toilet. I brushed her teeth for her. Together, we got her into her nightgown. She lay down in bed, and I propped her arm on pillows. Once she was asleep, I called Klein.

"How is she?" he asked.

"Not good. I'm so glad I'm here."

I made myself a drink, turned on the TV, and fell asleep in Daddy's chair.

The next morning, I woke early and went to check on her. She was in bed, staring at the ceiling.

"I think I need to go to a nursing home," she said. "I can't even go to the bathroom by myself."

After I'd fixed some coffee and gotten Mom set up in the sun-room, I called Barbara.

"She's pathetic," I said. "Not at all like Mom. All the fight's gone out of her. It's scary. Once I leave, you might have to come for few days."

She said she would, but I could almost hear her steeling herself.

For the next three days, Mom was listless and let me be in charge. I called doctors, took her for a follow-up clinic visit, and made sure she got a sling. I helped her figure out how to wipe her butt with her left hand. I gave her sponge baths until she was strong enough to stand in the shower with her cast wrapped in plastic. I made comfort food—grilled sandwiches for lunch and roast chicken for dinner. After a couple of days, her spirits improved, but that giant cast on her good arm prevented her from doing much on her own.

I called Barbara again.

"She's better, but she can't shower or dress by herself, and she needs help getting meals."

"I can come for a few days," said Barbara, "But then what? Can we get some home health care or something?"

What hadn't I thought of that? I knew all about home care. Medicare would pay if Mom was homebound, which she definitely was—and if she had a doctor's order, which I was sure I could get.

"I'll make some calls and get it set up." I said. "Maybe you won't have to come."

"No, I'm coming. I want to do my part."

I gave her a lot of credit. I knew spending a week with Mom wasn't high on her list, especially when Mom wasn't at her best.

Barbara flew in on Saturday, and I left on Sunday. She met with the home care nurse who came do the assessment. She made sure everything was set for Mom to get morning and evening visits, and stocked the freezer with home-cooked food that Mom could just warm up in the microwave or the oven.

When I called Tuesday night, Barbara said Mom was getting to be herself again, taking charge of everything.

"She asked me to write the monthly check for the condo fees, and talked me through it like I was a four-year-old. She pointed to the top line and said, 'Put the date here.'"

Over the next few months, Mom healed well, and after a grueling stretch of physical therapy, regained full use of her arm and wrist. I knew things were back to normal when she told me her ideas for the next editorial in *The Comet*.

Chapter 4

"I GUESS THAT WAS OUR REHEARSAL for her old age," Barbara said, once Mom had recovered from her broken wrist.

"I hate that thought, but I fear you're right. It was like she aged ten years after the fall. Thank goodness she bounced back."

If it was a rehearsal, I thought we'd done pretty well, but it bothered me that Mom had been alone the whole day before I arrived. And what if she had fallen at home instead of in the doctor's office? I did a half-hearted Internet search for information on those buttons you push to call for help if you fall and can't get up.

"Do you think we should talk to Mom about getting a panic button?" I asked Barbara.

She reminded me that Mom was back to all her usual activities, and wasn't even home that much. It was almost as if that acute attack of aging had granted her an immunity to growing older.

"How lucky are we that Mom is so independent?" I asked Barbara every time we talked over the next several years.

"Very lucky," she replied.

Three years after the broken wrist, around the time Mom turned eighty-five, Barbara and Phil bought a home in New Bern, North Carolina, a small town near the Eastern shore. They still lived in Arlington, but spent long weekends at the new house whenever they could. Phil loved the sailing community there, and he and Barbara were both tiring of the hustle and traffic around Washington, D.C. They planned to move to New Bern full-time in a few years, after Phil retired from his job as Director of Photographic Services at the American Red Cross.

Once they had a guest room set up, Barbara invited Mom and me to come see the house. I called Mom to coordinate travel plans. I was surprised when she said she was nervous about the trip and asked me to buy her ticket for her. She'd never been worried about traveling before.

"Mom, do you want me to meet you at the Tampa airport, so we can fly together?"

"Would you? It's not too much trouble?"

Flying from Miami through Tampa to get to North Carolina was a bit of a pain, but it was clear she wanted this, so I accepted the assignment without question. I was actually kind of grateful to be asked to do something for her.

"I'll arrange it," I said, "and we can meet at the ticket counter. Okay?"

"Yes. Good. I can get to the airport by myself." I could hear the relief in her voice.

Barbara's house was in an older neighborhood, where comfortable three-bedroom ranch homes like Barbara and Phil's faced super-sized houses that backed up to the Neuse River. It was April, and every yard featured a blooming dogwood or redbud tree along with bright swaths of colorful rhododendrons and azaleas. Mom and I sat in the back seat of the Honda, *oohing* and *aahing* as Barbara toured us around.

New Bern had been named by Swiss and German settlers after Bern, Switzerland. *Bern* is the German word for bear, and several corners of the city sported colorful fiberglass bear statues decorated by local artists.

On our way to the quaint town center for a bear tour and lunch in a rooftop garden, Mom pointed to an attractive brick building identified by a sign that read "McCarthy Court."

"Maybe I'll live there one day," Mom said.

"What are you talking about?" I asked. "What is it?"

"I don't know, but it looks like a nursing home." Mom faced front again as McCarthy Court receded behind us.

I twisted around in my seat, trying to get a better view of the building. I couldn't picture lively, active Mom in a nursing home anytime soon—or, really, ever. Besides, I had always assumed she would eventually live near me, not Barbara, and I was sure Barbara assumed the same.

"Oh, Mom, you're years away from anything like that," I said, trying to shake the whole thing off.

"I hope so," she said.

After the trip, I kept replaying the scene in my head.

In my hospice work, I had done research on causes of death and the use of healthcare services. I knew that, at eighty-five, Mom was in the category called "the oldest old," but she would also be regarded as "successfully aging," meaning that she was functioning well on every level—physically, mentally, and socially.

"What did you think about Mom noticing that nursing home?" I asked Barbara on a phone call shortly after the visit.

"It was weird. She seems just the same to me. Still giving me grief about my housekeeping and telling me how to cook the string beans."

Barb and I didn't call each other often, but when we did, we would always talk about how well Mom was doing at taking care of herself. One of us would express surprise and gratitude that there hadn't been a single crisis since the broken wrist. The other would say that it couldn't last forever. And then we'd go back to our everyday lives.

Two years after our first visit, Mom and I took a second trip to New Bern, for the October mum festival. Once again, I made all the arrangements, and this time, I even went to the condo for a night—both before and after the trip—at Mom's request. She said she didn't want to have to go to the airport alone. I barely registered Mom's request as a sign of her decline; instead, I felt happy about giving her some support.

We toured the neighborhoods, just as we had done on our first visit. This time, the trees were dressed in the reds and golds of fall. As Barbara drove us around, the talk was about recent events, and when Barbara and Phil might move to New Bern permanently. Even though Mom was now eighty-seven, the topic of nursing homes never came up.

A year later, in November, 2004, Barbara and I visited Mom in New Port Richey to celebrate my fifty-second birthday. We invited Ginny and Lenore to join us for dinner at Bon Appétit in Dunedin. As the waitress brought our drinks, Ginny mentioned that her daughter and son-in-law were moving back to Florida to be closer to her.

"I never want to live with either one of my girls," Mom said.

"Mom! That sounds awful," I scolded her from across the table.

"Well, you know what I mean. I just don't want to be a burden."

I made my usual speech about how taking care of your family is not a burden. "It may not be easy, and it may not be fun, but it's what families do."

Mom said, "Anyway, I'm going to stay in my condo until I die."

We'd had this conversation before, and it made me angry.

"Why does she say those things?" I asked Barbara later that night. "Of course, we're going to take care of her, whatever that entails."

"It's not about us," Barbara said. "It's about her, about staying in control. What she really means is that she never wants to be dependent on us, or on anyone."

Barbara was right. I had missed that nuance, but she hadn't.

I wondered whether Mom's hopes of staying in her condo until she died were realistic. And I also wondered what had happened to her noble, if surprising, comments about moving to a nursing home.

Two months later, in January, 2005, I went back to New Port Richey to celebrate Mom's birthday. She was turning eighty-nine.

Just as she had done on almost all my visits, Mom reminded me about the preparations for her death: the will, the trust, and the living will.

"Remember, I don't want any heroics," she would say. "When it's time, you have to let me go. No surgeries or chemotherapy. No hospitals."

She'd had the few antiques she owned appraised. She'd made lists of the china, silverware, and family heirlooms, so Barb and I could choose what we wanted. And she reminded me, yet again, about the memorial service.

"Speak up so everyone can hear you!"

She was preparing for her death, but she wasn't dying. She wasn't even sick. Still, her preparations made me feel like I should be preparing, too. With all my hospice experience, I was pretty sure I would know what to do when she really was dying. I had a vague notion that there would be some stage between how it was now and how it would be when she was dying, but I remained halfway stuck in my myth that she would go suddenly, like Daddy. How could I prepare for that?

Then I received a letter from Lenore, who was now eighty-one years old.

Your mother is slowing down, and eventually, she will need more help, she wrote. *I know you want to do what is best for her.* Lenore was encouraging Mom to think about moving nearer to either Barbara or me.

I was mortified that Lenore felt she had to write this letter. I thought I'd been paying attention. What important cue had I missed? How could it suddenly be time for her to move? I called Barbara.

"I've been watching her," I said. "She seems fine. What am I missing?"

"Well, you did have to go over and travel with her last time you came here."

"Yes, but travel is hard for everybody since 9-11," I reasoned.

"She told me she's starting to limit her driving, to short distances and places she knows well," Barbara said.

"Listen, that's why they call it 'aging well,'" I argued. "She's being sensible, and adapting to getting older."

"Yes, but it also means she's doing less, and maybe getting more isolated."

"Do you think so?" It was hard for me to see Mom as needy; I didn't want to see her that way. "Well, whatever it is, Lenore thinks Mom needs help, so I'm going to go see for myself," I told Barbara.

I called Mom. She always gave me grief when I wanted to fly over just to visit her, so my plan was to lie about having business with the local hospice. In the first moments of the conversation, even before I brought up the subject of a visit, she told me she had an appointment to have her cataracts removed. It was the perfect excuse.

"I'll come over and go with you." I said.

"You don't need to do that. They have a van that picks you up and drives you home."

"But what about when you get home? Are you having both eyes done?"

"They do them about two weeks apart. I'll be fine." Mom did not seem concerned.

"Mom, I really want to come, at least for the first eye."

"Well, if you want to come, come. I always love to see you."

I wrote back to Lenore. *I'm so grateful you contacted me. I'm going to visit Mom next month and talk to her about moving.*

As I wrote, I thought about how Mom had been all set to have cataract surgery by herself. To me, that looked like one more piece of evidence that she was still doing fine.

I looked at Lenore's letter to me, and mine to her, lying open on my desk. We were two people who loved Mom, with two very different interpretations of her situation. I needed to get to the truth.

I arrived at about noon, and after a quick sandwich, Mom and I went to the eye clinic for the pre-op exam. I was freaked out when they propped her eye open to take some measurements, but she swore it didn't hurt at all. She was completely calm. I was not.

That evening, we went out to Carrabba's for dinner. It was still light out, so I let Mom drive. She went too slowly on the highway, but it wasn't scary.

We sat down and ordered our usual cocktails. Mostly because I had told Lenore I would, I brought up the subject of moving.

"Have you thought any more about moving nearer to either Barbara or me?"

I was trying to be fair, and not just assume that Mom would end up near me, but I thought that was what would happen—and that was what I wanted.

"Yes, I've been talking to Lenore about it," Mom said.

"So, what are you thinking?"

"Well, I'm not going anytime soon, but when I'm ready, I'll probably go to North Carolina, to that place near Barbara," she said.

I sipped my Manhattan and leaned back in the booth, trying not to look shocked or offended. *This is about what Mom wants*, I told myself.

"Really?" I said. "Why not Miami?"

"Mel, you're never there. You travel all the time. Why would I want to be in Miami without you?"

That hurt. Did she think I wouldn't take care of her?

"Well, if you moved there, I wouldn't travel all the time. I *would* be around."

Until that moment, I hadn't thought about the rearrangements that would be needed. I was sure I could make it work if I had to.

She said, "You can't change your whole life like that. I wouldn't want you to. You love your work."

"Well, I love you more," I said, "and I am going to look into options in Miami. But I'll ask Barbara to get some information on McCarthy Court, too."

Mom sailed through the cataract surgery in great good humor. She insisted she'd go alone for the second eye. For my entire two-day visit, she had been completely self-sufficient, fixing her own breakfast, dressing, and even driving.

It didn't make sense. Lenore was smart and she knew Mom well, so I couldn't just discount her perspective. But it didn't add up for me.

The day after the Mom's surgery, I was scheduled to drive down the west coast of Florida from New Port Richey to Bonita Springs, to meet Klein at a new Hyatt hotel for a weekend vacation. I had a three-hour trip, and it was the perfect time to really think things through. I left Mom's, went to Starbucks for an iced espresso, and got on the highway.

I thought about what Lenore had written—that Mom was slowing down. I agreed with that, but mostly, I was impressed with how much she was still doing. What did Lenore see that I didn't? She'd said Mom would need more help. I agreed with that, too, but we weren't there yet.

I turned on the car radio. NPR was reporting on Hurricane Dennis. It had hit Navarre Beach along the northwest coast of Florida, near Pensacola, just a few days before. There had been forty-two deaths. I had lived in Florida for over twenty years. I knew you had to prepare for the worst way ahead of time, when the hurricane was still over the mid-Atlantic, even before the forecasters could tell you which way it would go. I knew you couldn't wait until the wind was high and scary to evacuate—because then it was too late. I started to see Lenore as my personal NOAA, warning me about Hurricane Mom. Even though the water had barely started to rise, the floods were coming, and it might get deep fast.

Mom, me, and Barbara in Barbara and Phil's house in New Bern. My brother-in-law, Phil, took this in 2008 and entitled it "Pratts in a Row."

Chapter 5

I CALLED BARBARA and told her about my pitiful epiphany.

"How could it be such a shock to me that Mom is old? She's eighty-nine!"

"Because she doesn't want us to think she's old." Barbara's voice was calm.

"Is it a shock to you?"

"No. I've just been pretending."

I got on the computer and typed "senior living Miami" into Google. I was aware of two possible options: "life care" communities and nursing homes. In my hospice work, I had visited lots of nursing homes, and I'd always had to steel myself. I'd paint on a smile and force cheerful greetings for the residents, who were bedbound or getting around in wheelchairs. No matter how hard the administration tried to make the homes look good, they remained gray and depressing, mostly because the residents were in bad shape and needed full-time nursing care. Mom didn't belong in a nursing home.

I had also visited my father's cousin, Gratia, after she had moved to a life care community on a large wooded campus outside Philadelphia. The year she'd moved in, she had paid an "entry fee" of almost $50,000—about what a small house cost at the time. She also paid monthly rent, for a two-bedroom apartment which she filled with her favorite antiques—including a maple dresser and bedside table that are now in my home in Florida—and her four-poster bed that was so tall she needed a step stool to climb in. Gratia lived completely independently for several years, then added a meal plan and had dinner in the communal dining room. When she got to the point where she needed more help, she transferred to what they called personal care—a single room, three meals a day, and help with dressing and medications as needed. Toward the end, when her congestive heart failure got worse and her memory failed, she was transferred to the nursing home on the same campus. Her monthly payments had gone up with each transfer, but the initial buy-in fee entitled her to care for as long as she needed it, even if she ran out of money. I supposed something like that might work for Mom.

I found two life care communities in the Miami area, and both were all wrong. First of all, they were expensive, with buy-in fees of close to $100,000. Even with the guarantee of perpetual care, I knew Mom would never go for it. Though she could afford it, she preferred to live modestly. She just didn't spend that kind of money on anything. Then there was the geography. The one closest to me was still forty-five minutes away, and way too fancy. Mom was not the crystal chandelier and French provincial furniture type. The place where I thought she would fit in best was well over an hour from my house, which didn't accomplish the primary goal of having Mom "near" me.

I was also concerned about Miami's culture. Mom had spent the last thirty-five years of her life in New Port Richey, where most people are from the Midwest. I knew it would be hard, if not impossible, for her adapt to caregivers who barely spoke English and the *mañana* attitude of the tropics.

I told Mom that I really wanted her to move near me, but that I was having trouble finding good options for senior living in Miami.

She said, "Mel, I already told you. If I move, I'm going to New Bern."

It made me nervous that she said "if."

While I had been striking out in Miami, Barbara had struck gold in New Bern. She sent me a brochure on McCarthy Court, the place

Mom had pointed out on our first trip to North Carolina. It wasn't a nursing home; it was an adult congregate living facility. I'd heard the term—ACLF—but knew nothing about how they worked. According to the brochure, McCarthy Court offered one- and two-bedroom apartments for monthly rental, with no buy-in fee and no lease. The seniors playing bridge and enjoying dinner in the pictures were probably actors, but they looked so healthy and happy. I wanted to believe they loved it at McCarthy Court. Apartments came with light housekeeping once a week, and daily check-ins to be sure everyone was still breathing. (Push the button in the bathroom by 10 A.M., or somebody comes to check on you.) Residents had dinner together in the communal dining room. McCarthy provided shuttle service to shopping and doctor's appointments, and they offered field trips to museums, plays, and concerts. Next door to McCarthy, and under the same management, was Homeplace, an assisted-living facility. If necessary, Mom could move across the parking lot to the higher level of care. All that, and Barbara's house was only five minutes away. Another similar option, The Villages, was just ten minutes from the house. It all sounded too good to be true. Why wasn't there anything like this near me?

"I don't understand what's happening," I told Klein. "I always thought I'd be the one to take care of Mom, but now she says she'd rather be in New Bern, and there are great places for her there and nothing here." I heard myself whining.

"And I can't imagine her living with us," I said, hoping he would ask, "Why not?" Hoping that maybe it was possible.

Klein was more in Barbara's camp than mine when it came to Mom. He loved her because she was my mother, but he found her annoying. He disliked her verbal aggression. If you didn't agree with her, she'd explain it all again; clearly, you hadn't understood her the first time. He said it felt like she was attacking him. He hated it even more when she criticized me, telling me I worked too hard, or that I would look better in brighter colors. I didn't feel criticized. That was just how Mom and I talked to each other, but I liked that he felt protective.

"Mel, if it has to be, then it has to be," he said, "but it doesn't sound like that's what she wants."

He was right. It wasn't what she wanted. She'd made it clear she wanted to live on her own, and if she couldn't stay in Florida, she wanted to move near Barbara.

At the time, I didn't even think about why Mom had been so set on New Bern. Today, I wonder. Was she thinking of me and how much it would change my life? Or was she thinking that maybe this was her last chance to finally get into Barbara's life?

Whatever it was, I knew I had to give up on Miami. Klein would have put up with Mom, but I knew how he really felt. I loved them both, but they were like oil and water. I would have torn myself apart trying to make them both happy.

I called Mom to plan another trip to North Carolina, and tried to sound casual about the plan to look at new places to live. I expected resistance.

"Barbara will set up visits to both McCarthy Court and The Villages, just to see what's out there," I said.

"Good. I might be moving sooner than you think."

"Really? Like when?" I asked.

"Maybe sometime next year."

What? I thought. Did I hear that right? Less than two months earlier, she hadn't been ready at all. I didn't ask why she had changed her mind. I didn't want to dissuade her in any way.

"Okay, then, let's go to New Bern." I tried to sound cheerful.

I poured myself some Lillet and sat on the porch watching the reflected glow of the sunset on the houses across the bay. It was beautiful, but Mom would not be seeing it. I prayed that the places in New Bern would be nice, that Mom would like them, that she would be happy. I prayed for a sign that the trip to New Bern was the right thing to do.

Both McCarthy Court and The Villages surprised me. At both places, the apartments were cheerful, spacious, and homey, not anything like an "institution." As we walked around, people would stop us, ask Mom if she was thinking of moving in, and say how much they loved it there. I started thinking there was something in the water. I expected old people who were confused, and maybe in wheelchairs. Though we saw lots of canes and walkers, these folks moved. We saw bridge groups and men shooting pool. We did not see anyone playing shuffleboard. I thought I'd have to look hard for the pros, and was prepared to downplay the cons. I didn't have to do either.

At The Villages, all the apartment doors opened onto a small campus. The wide concrete walkways were lined with flowering shrubs, and there were several small park-like areas with benches and crepe myrtle trees. The parking lot was behind the buildings, and it looked like many of the residents had cars.

McCarthy Court was a three-story building with each apartment opening onto a wide, well-lit hallway with hardwood floors. The first floor smelled faintly of pine-scented cleaner. Paintings, mostly landscapes, hung high on the walls, and when I looked carefully, I noticed that the decorative molding halfway up was actually a railing you could grab if you needed to steady yourself. I was impressed. So was Mom.

"I could live in either one of those places," she said, "But I like McCarthy Court better."

Barbara and I agreed that McCarthy seemed more homey.

"Mom, I can't believe you spotted it four years ago!" I was excited.

She said, "It just looked like a nice place."

Mom went to bed right after dinner. It was only 8:00 P.M. Barbara and I took our books and some wine out to the wrought iron table on her little screened patio.

"I can't believe this is going so well." I said.

"Do you really think she might move here?" Barbara asked.

"After today, it sure seems like it."

Barbara stared out into the dark back yard. "Yeah, I guess it does."

The next day, I got up early and went jogging. As my feet ran on the pavement, possible scenarios for Mom ran through my head.

We had about seven months before Barb and Phil were selling their Arlington house and moving to New Bern full time. We could wait until then to put Mom's name on the list for McCarthy Court. They had told us it usually took three to six months for an apartment to come available. That would work.

I decided to add an extra mile to my circuit. Joni Mitchell sang "Lucky Girl" through my iPod, and I sang along.

I'm a lucky girl
I found my friend
I've been all around the world
Mission Impossible
Chasing the rainbow's end.

I was feeling good. McCarthy Court was perfect, and Mom was on board. I had heard the horror stories about parents who refused to move out of their homes, or have any help come in. Their children, my friends, worried all the time. We were going to avoid all that. Mom would be moving before she really started to go downhill. Man, we were lucky!

As I slowed up to make the turn back toward the house, it suddenly occurred to me that this lovely scenario might not be feeling so perfect to Barbara and Phil. When they had bought this place, I was sure they'd seen it as a getaway, a place for a slower, more carefree life. Taking on Mom would not be carefree, and I knew it wasn't part of the plan.

Barbara was outside pulling weeds when I got back.

"Where's Mom?" I asked.

"Taking a shower."

"Barb, I just realized what having Mom in New Bern will mean for you and Phil."

Barbara grabbed the hand hoe and stabbed at the ground.

"I know, it's not what any of us had planned," she said.

"Is Phil okay with it, if it happens?"

"Yeah, he'll be okay. We both wish it was you, instead, but we get it."

"I'm sorry I didn't think about this before."

"It's alright. I've thought about it enough for both of us."

Four months later, in January 2006, Mom turned ninety. We planned a birthday dinner for her at Bon Appétit, and invited her friends Jane and Bill Johnson along with Lenore and Ginny.

I wandered into Mom's room as we were dressing to go out. I always liked to poke through her jewelry to see if anything went with my outfit. She was sitting on a chair and pulling on her nylon knee-highs. She picked up the stocking and rolled it down from the top edge, using both hands, then, reaching her arms out, bent over as far as she could. Barely lifting her foot off the floor, she fitted the stocking toe over her toes, and slowly rolled it up to her knee. The right leg took a full minute. I sat on the bed with the jewelry box beside me. Out of the corner of my eye, I watched her do the left leg—another full minute.

The restaurant was loud, and it was hard to hear across the large round table. I sat next to Bill Johnson. He was a talker, regaling us with funny stories about his years in the Foreign Service. I kept my eye on Mom, but never caught a glimpse of that old woman who had taken so long to pull on her knee-highs. Instead, she ordered her usual martini and half-rack of lamb, rare. She ate everything. She laughed at Bill's stories, and threatened us with walking out if we dared to sing "Happy Birthday." We settled for a toast to her health. *May it last, at least until we get her settled in New Bern*, I thought.

The next day, Mom was up early, making coffee and cutting up fresh fruit for us. Barbara and I were in vacation mode. We took our time reading the paper, and went for a long walk. Off and on during the day, all three of us worked at the *New York Times* crossword puzzle. After lunch, Mom napped a little in Daddy's chair in the sunroom. Barbara and I did some grocery shopping. We bought a chicken and lots of fresh vegetables to cook for dinner plus leftovers, and some frozen entrées for later in the week.

Over cocktails, I steered the conversation to New Bern.

"Hey, Mom, Barb and Phil will be moving to New Bern soon." I poked at the cherry in my Manhattan. "Maybe you should go ahead and put your name on the list for McCarthy Court."

"I don't know. I've been thinking I'd rather stay here."

Oh no, I thought. *Please don't do this.* I concentrated on sounding unconcerned.

"I thought you liked McCarthy and New Bern." I said.

"I do. But I'm comfortable here."

"Now what?" I said to Barbara when we were alone in the kitchen.

"I don't know," she said. "There's no making Mom do something she doesn't want to do."

"No, but she must see that this is going to happen, right? I mean, she's smart, right? She just needs some encouragement, right?"

Barbara finished carving the chicken, and started serving up three plates.

"Not too much for me," I said. "I'm not very hungry."

In the months following her birthday, Mom seemed like a marathon runner who had used up her last ounce of energy to get across the finish line. She cut back to playing bridge once a week. She resigned as historian of her university women's group. She told me the guy who invented television was her hero, because the "boob tube" kept her company all day long. It was as if suddenly, at age ninety, her switch had flipped from "on" to "old."

She had talked about giving up *The Comet* for a year or two, but hadn't found anyone to take it on. Amazingly, she was still putting together every issue. Then, in April, about three months after her birthday, she told me she was resigning.

"I let the condo board know I'm serious this time," she said, "They need to find a new editor, and soon."

"Mom, are you sad? Or will it be a relief to give it up?"

"Both. But, I can't keep it up. It's too much for me now."

"I'm really proud of you, Mom, for all those years you did a great job, and for knowing when it was time to stop." I kept my voice calm.

Then, later that evening, when I told Klein about it, I cried.

Chapter 6

Most days, I called Mom mid-morning, after Klein had left for his office and I had finished my forty minutes on the elliptical trainer. I swiveled my office chair toward the window, took a deep breath, and hit #1 on the speed dial.

I started every call the same way. "Hey, Mom, how're you doing?"

If she said, "Pretty good for an old lady," I'd relax a little, knowing she was having a good day. We'd talk about what we were reading, or who she had seen at the grocery store, or her bridge game.

Once she quit *The Comet*, her answer was more often a downbeat "Okay." We'd talk about how she was napping more, going to bed right after *Wheel of Fortune* and then waking up at 4:00 in the morning.

"I get up, make coffee and toast, and then work on the crossword puzzle. Sometimes, I go back to bed for a nap around 8:00."

Those days, my phone felt like it weighed twenty pounds.

Every couple of weeks, I'd bring up McCarthy Court, and urge her to get on the waiting list. She'd say she was just fine where she was.

But she wasn't fine, and neither was I. One day, I called six times over about four hours, and got a constant busy signal. Every time I dialed, my blood pressure went up a notch. It wasn't her day for bridge. Where could she be? I imagined her trapped in her car in a ditch somewhere along Route 19, or lying on the bathroom floor with her beautiful white hair hardened in a pool of blood. Unable to concentrate on work, I called Ginny and asked her to check on Mom.

I grabbed the phone on the first ring. "I'm fine, I'm fine," Mom said, "Somehow the phone got cockeyed on the cradle. Usually it makes that *be-doo, be-doo* sound, but I never heard it."

A month or so later, it happened again—a busy signal for hours, an apologetic call to Ginny to ask for help again, and the phone was off the hook. This time, I was angry. How could she be so careless? Didn't she understand how I worried?

I told Mom, "If you're not ready to move, then at least you have to get one of those buttons you can push for help."

She reluctantly agreed, but two weeks went by, and she hadn't called the 800 number I had given her to place the order. I checked with Barbara to be sure she would back me up.

"One hundred percent," she said.

I signed Mom up for the service, had the equipment shipped to her house, and booked a flight over. Mom was not delighted.

"I'm fine," she whined. "I do not need this."

"I need it," I said. "I worry about you more than you want me to."

The equipment consisted of a single beige box, about eight-inches square with a big red button in the middle. It was basically a speaker-phone that automatically dialed the monitoring company when any of the panic buttons—the one on the box or the ones on the wrist-band or neck pendant—were pushed. I studied the diagram in the instruction book, and realized it hooked up exactly like a telephone answering machine. Mom's phone sat on top of the upright piano in the living room. I moved some of the family pictures aside to make room for the plastic box. Five minutes after I had started setting up the system, I pushed the button to test it.

"Connect America," said the voice coming from the speaker.

"Hi," I said, "We're just testing the equipment."

"Is this Mrs. Pratt?" said the voice.

Mom shouted, "I'm right here."

Then she whispered to me, "How do they know it's me?" I explained they could see her name and phone number on a computer monitor.

I told the voice I wanted to do a test from the bedroom to make sure Mom could communicate with them from there. It worked perfectly.

Mom and I put the wrist-banded button on the bedside table, and I put the one on the lanyard around her neck.

"It's ugly," she said. I told her to tuck it under her blouse.

I made her promise to wear it for a week. I hoped it would become habit to put it on in the morning and take it off at night, when she would have the bedside one.

"Wear it in the shower. It's designed to get wet." I was as firm as I'd ever been with her.

Then we went out to dinner.

When the waitress asked for our drink orders, Mom said, "I'll have a glass of Chardonnay. Martinis seem to hit me too hard these days."

I looked at Mom over the top of my menu.

"I'll have the same," I said.

I swallowed hard. She was still my smart mother if she knew enough to give up her beloved cocktail.

Two weeks later, Mom called me at 7:00 A.M.

"Don't worry. Everything's fine," she said.

She told me she'd gotten up at 4:30 and gone into the kitchen for some orange juice when she started to feel lightheaded. She had eased herself down to sit on the floor, and then realized she couldn't get up.

"I felt so stupid," she said.

"No, you were smart to sit down." My heart pounded, and I had to sit down right on the floor next to the phone. Klein brought me a chair. I stayed where I was, and grabbed his hand.

"I needed help, so I pushed the button." Mom sounded calm. I was shaking.

She told the voice on the intercom to call the office and tell the security guard to come by.

"He was here in less than five minutes, and helped me up. This button thing is great!" She was giddy. Finally, I laughed.

At first, I felt like we had dodged a bullet. Then I worried that this would make her feel more secure and less like moving. Maybe a few hours alone on the kitchen floor would have convinced her to make the commitment to McCarthy Court.

We were teetering on an edge here, and I didn't know how to find the right balancing point.

Lenore's second letter came about six months after Mom's ninetieth birthday. I had to read it twice. She used the words "depression" and "loss of weight" and "confusion." She explained that she now had a standing date to take Mom to dinner once a week, and that Ginny brought Mom food every couple of days—otherwise, they worried she "might not eat." She wrote that Mom's friends wouldn't ride in the car when Mom drove. She described how Mom was losing her skills for playing bridge.

No one really wants to play with her anymore, Lenore wrote. My heart broke for Mom.

My hands were clammy, and my head ached. I took some ibuprofen and made myself a cappuccino. Then I read the letter again, and cried. I called Barbara, but she wasn't home. I called Klein at work.

"How could things have deteriorated that much? I just saw her a couple of months ago, when I put in the panic button," I sobbed.

"I don't know, honey. Why don't you call Lenore? I think it's pretty clear that she wants to help."

For work, I have a twenty-four-hour rule—don't react to something that seems calamitous for a full day. The potential to make things worse is highest when I'm all wrought up, and good solutions come to me after I've had time to calm down. I couldn't bear to wait twenty-four hours to call Lenore, but I did wait until later in the evening, when I could talk without crying.

I told her I was grateful she had written. She said she hoped I didn't feel she was meddling.

"I had no idea things had gotten so bad," I said, "She seemed alright last time I visited."

"She rallies when you're around. Then she needs several days to recover."

I filled her in on Mom's reluctance to get on the waiting list for McCarthy Court. I told her Mom had talked about finding a place like McCarthy right there in New Port Richey.

"I know," said Lenore, "but I don't think it's a good idea. You and Barbara will be too far away."

She told me other women in their group had moved to senior apartments in the area, and none of the local friends ever visited. "She's too isolated in her condo, and she'd be even more isolated in a senior apartment here in New Port Richey," Lenore said.

Then she said the one thing I feared most.

"I think you will have to make this decision for her. She can't do it."

Mom's independence, her autonomy, was so important to her. I respected Lenore, but I wasn't ready to accept the idea that Mom could not make this decision. I called two of Mom's other friends. They confirmed everything Lenore had said. They had heard about McCarthy Court from Mom, and said it sounded perfect. Both of them told me that Mom was probably too scared of moving to pull the trigger, and that I would have to help her.

Barbara wanted to go ahead and put Mom on the waiting list without even telling her, and tried to reason with me. "It could be a while before her name comes up."

"I know," I said, "but I just can't do it."

I knew that committing to McCarthy Court was a huge decision—and I was still determined to try to make it Mom's decision, rather than Barbara's or mine. Mom wasn't demented or incompetent. It was becoming clear, however, that she was depressed.

Barbara, Mom, and I all had experience with depression. Mom had suffered debilitating postpartum depression when I was born.

During my sophomore year of high school, I slept fifteen hours a day. I knew exactly how dark and hopeless the days are when you're depressed, how exhausted you feel all the time, without even the energy to brush your teeth. Barbara's depression coincided with her first panic attacks, when she became housebound, too enervated to get out the door on her own.

We had all bounced back. Now, Mom faced the demon again. I thought maybe if we could get her feeling better, she would see that moving to New Bern was the logical choice.

I suggested she make a doctor's appointment. I urged her to tell Dr. G. that she'd been feeling tired, and had given up a lot of her usual activities.

"You seem depressed," I said. "Maybe he could give you some medication."

Mom didn't argue. In fact, she thought it was a good idea. She called Dr. G. as soon as we hung up, and within a few days, she started taking both an antidepressant and an antianxiety medication.

More and more often, the answer to "How're you doing?" was "Pretty good for an old lady." I knew she was eating better, because when I asked what she'd had for lunch, she'd tell me rather than saying, "I wasn't hungry."

After she had been taking the medication, for about a month, I emailed Lenore and asked if she'd seen any change. She replied that Mom definitely seemed to have more energy. She also made it clear that moving was still the best, if not the only, option.

I called Mom and told her I was coming to visit, specifically so we could call Diane at McCarthy Court together and then send the deposit to get on the waiting list.

"No, let's go to New Bern instead." Mom said she felt more positive about moving, but she wanted to see it one more time before making the final decision.

I flew to New Port Richey a day early, and helped Mom pack for the short trip. I fixed two turkey sandwiches to eat on the airplane. I wrapped the sandwiches in wax paper and thought about all those days when I had been too anxious to eat breakfast, and Mom would wrap up a half-piece of toast for me to have at recess.

At the airport, I pulled up to the departure curb and took Mom and her suitcase inside. I found her a seat, and told her to wait while I parked the car. It took me about fifteen minutes to park and walk back to the terminal with my bag. Mom hadn't moved. She still had one hand on her suitcase. I touched her arm.

"Ready?" I asked, smiling.

"Ready or not," she said.

Mom started to wilt in the security line. One of the airline representatives noticed, and waved us over.

"Come this way," she said, and led us through the entrance for handicapped passengers.

Our flight from Tampa left late, so we had only thirty minutes to make our connection in Charlotte. The gates for the smaller regional planes were a long walk from the gate where we had landed from Tampa. I knew Mom would never make it in time. I told the airline agent we needed a ride. She said we had to wait for one of the courtesy carts to come by, and flag it down.

"What about a wheelchair?" I asked.

She said it had to be reserved ahead of time.

I got Mom settled in a seat, and we both had a few sips from our bottle of spring water. Then I walked into the middle of the concourse to look for a cart. There were none in sight. Five minutes went by. My armpits were soaking wet. I wanted to run to the next gate and have them hold the plane, but I couldn't leave Mom. Five more minutes passed. Finally, a courtesy cart came by, going the wrong way. I stopped the driver, and made him promise to pick up Mom on his way back. I told him our connecting gate number, and gave him a $20 tip in advance.

"Just wait here for the cart," I told Mom, "I'm going to go to the next gate and make sure they know we're coming."

"Where do I go?" Mom asked. She was about to cry.

"It's gate E-21. The driver knows. It's going to be alright. I won't let them leave without us."

I grabbed both of our bags, wheeling one in front and pulling one behind me. As I ran to the gate, Mom passed by on the cart, but she didn't see me. I got to the gate just as the driver was helping her down. There was no one there but the ticket agent, and they were about to close the door to the jet bridge.

"Did my daughter get on the plane?" Mom asked.

"It's okay, Mom. I'm right here," I said.

As she turned toward me, she looked as if she had aged ten years in the last ten minutes.

We boarded, and I held her hand as the plane sped down the runway.

Chapter 7

NEW BERN BLESSED US with two beautiful Indian summer days. The foliage around McCarthy court was lush. Inside, the pale green walls were soothing. Diane, the director, suggested we sit in the dining room. She led Mom, Barbara, and me to a table that would seat six. From there, we could look out a huge bank of windows into the main hallway. I watched a few gray heads wander by and peek in to see what was going on. Diane asked one of the servers setting tables to bring us some iced tea.

"Could I have coffee, instead?" Mom asked.

"Sure, honey," said the server, "I'm Christine. You want anything else, you let me know. Okay?"

I was checking things off my mental list: friendly staff, clean tablecloths, comfortable chairs, not too formal.

Diane explained that none of the apartments were vacant, but two of the residents had invited us to see us their places. She showed us drawings of the floor plans.

"What else would you like to see?" she asked. We all looked at Mom.

"What else is there?" Mom asked.

Diane suggested we visit the bar first, then see the recreation areas after our tour of the apartments. Mom nodded.

The "bar" turned out to be a six-by-eight-foot room with two tables where residents could have a cocktail before dinner. Diane gestured toward the cupboards, and explained that people kept their own liquor bottles there and the staff would mix drinks for them. On Fridays, everyone was invited to have a glass of wine during happy hour, but no liquor was allowed in the dining room. Mom said she would probably have some Chardonnay in her room before dinner with some crackers and cheese. I loved how it seemed like she could see herself living there.

We took the elevator to the second floor and met Mrs. James, who showed us around her two-bedroom apartment. She had furnished it tastefully with Danish-style contemporary furniture. It felt stylish, if dated, and comfortable—much like Mom's condo.

"In Florida, I have a teak dining table from Scandinavian Design," Mom said, "but it would be too big to bring with me here."

The bathroom layout was ingeniously designed to accommodate two people sharing the apartment, though Mrs. James lived alone. There were two rooms, each with a toilet and sink. Doors from each of these rooms led to a central space containing a walk-in shower. Mrs. James said she had moved in two years ago, a few months after her husband had died. Her children lived about an hour away.

"Best decision I *evah* made," she said in her gentle Southern accent.

I gave Mom a squeeze.

Then we met Sophie. She had come to New Bern from New York years earlier, to be closer to her son. She told us she had trouble with her circulation.

"When my legs got bad," she said, "I moved to McCarthy."

Her apartment had only one bedroom, and was smaller than Mrs. James' place, but Sophie had packed it with at least twice as much furniture, including a small organ. It turned out she still worked as a church organist, and played piano for events at McCarthy, as well.

"Most of my things are still at my house. I can't bring myself to sell it." Sophie gestured for us to sit on the couch. "But I prefer living here. I like to be around people."

She used a walker, the kind with a seat and a basket. As we left her apartment, Barbara and I laughed, wondering how in the world she maneuvered her walker around all that stuff.

We took a quick tour of the recreation room, and looked at the calendar of monthly activities. There was something every day: bridge, morning coffee and donuts, a trip to the new museum with lunch at the café, van trips to the local supermarket on Mondays and Thursdays, a concert in the dining room, and more.

The three of us joined Diane in her small office. Barbara asked about the waiting list. Diane said they required a $500 deposit, but if you decided to take your name off the list, it would be refunded. It didn't sound like much of a commitment to me. I stayed quiet.

"How long is the list?" Mom asked. Diane said it might take about three to four months before there would be a vacancy.

"What if Mom's name comes up, and she's not ready to move?" I asked. Diane said Mom could just move down a slot and wait for the next opening.

No pressure at all, I thought.

We left and headed for a sandwich shop. Once we had our water and iced tea, I asked Mom what she thought.

"What's not to like?" she said. "The apartments are lovely. And I feel like I could be friends with both those people, though Sophie might be a lot to take."

Barbara and I laughed.

"Are you ready to sign up?" Barbara asked.

"I guess so," said Mom, "but I want to think about it for a day or two."

"Mom, it's never going to get easier to make this move," I said. "At some point, you just have to do it."

"I will, but not today."

The trip back to Florida was uneventful, but I could see that Mom was exhausted. I suggested staying with her another day or so.

"You should get home," she said. "You have work."

A few days after our trip, Mom called to say she had changed her mind.

"Maybe I'll move someday," she said, "but for now, I want to stay here."

I paced around my office.

"Mom, I really don't think that's practical."

"Mel, it's just too hard to think about moving."

I called Barbara.

"We have to take charge," I said. "I'll send you a check for half the deposit."

Barbara said, "She won't like it."

"I don't like it," I said. "Put her name on the list."

When I was young, doctor's and dentist's appointments were major triggers for my anxiety. Mom would never write the appointments on the Girl Scout calendar we kept on the desk in the kitchen, even though it was her primary scheduling tool. She knew I would start worrying weeks ahead of time. Instead, she'd wait until the day of the appointment, and tell me about it that morning. I'd still throw up, but at least I only had one day of anxiety.

In keeping the secret about putting her on the waiting list for McCarthy Court, I told myself I was returning the favor. Why worry her before the place became a real possibility? But it felt like a lie, and after a couple of months, I told her that Barbara was going to keep checking to see if anything was available at McCarthy Court.

"Okay, but I still haven't decided for sure about moving," Mom said.

"I know," I said, then changed the subject.

In January of 2007, Mom turned ninety-one. In March, Barbara got the call. Diane from McCarthy Court said there would be a two-bedroom apartment available in May.

Barbara and I tried to think of all the questions Mom would have, and what her objections might be. Barbara made sure to get all the basic information on the price and the lease. I checked with Keith, the financial advisor, and he confirmed that Mom had plenty of money for the move. If Mom was resistant, we would be firm.

I used three-way calling to get us all on the phone together.

"Mom, are you there?"

"Yes."

"Barb?"

"I'm here, too."

Barbara told Mom about the apartment.

"Yours would be like Mrs. James's place—the one with the pretty teak furniture," I said.

"Did she move?" Mom asked.

"No, she's still there. You wouldn't have her place, but yours would be the same floor plan," I explained.

"That place was pretty big. Do I need two bedrooms?" asked Mom.

"It's smaller than your place now, but you'd still be able to keep a lot of your furniture," Barbara said.

"Can I afford it?"

"Yes," I said. "If you're worried, talk to Keith at Smith-Barney."

"How would I get there?"

"Barbara and I will take care of all the arrangements," I said. I had been thinking that Barbara could fly down to Florida and take Mom back to her house for a week. I would stay behind and work with the movers.

"Melly and I really think you should take the apartment," Barbara said.

I was pacing back and forth in the Florida room. I swung the arm that wasn't holding the phone up and down, trying to shake off some of my anxiety. Barbara and I had to be what Mom had been for us— the ones who knew best. I hated it.

"Well, could I look at it again?" Mom said.

The idea of another trip made me feel sick, but she'd cracked the door a bit, and I pushed it open.

"Sure, we can go up next week." I said.

"That soon?" Mom asked.

"We have to decide right away," I said. "Other people are waiting."

What I wanted that day, that moment, was to jump on a plane and go to her. Instead, I called Lenore and let her know what was happening. She said she would call Mom a little later and see how she was doing. My shoulders came down about half an inch.

For the trip, I ordered a wheelchair for both the Tampa and Charlotte airports. Mom protested that she didn't need it. I told her it was a ruse to get through security faster, and to move to the front of the line for boarding the plane. I didn't tell her how worried I was about making our connection. I packed a lunch and snacks. I checked the bags in with the airline, something I never did on a business trip, and hoped they wouldn't get lost..

Our connecting flight out of Charlotte was delayed almost an hour. We had plenty of time for a bathroom break and a stop for a fresh bottle of water. Once we were organized in seats at the departure gate, I cracked open the water, took a sip, and passed it to Mom. She sat without moving, like someone in pain, and barely turned her head toward me.

"I don't know how you do all the traveling you do, Mel. It's so hard."

"We'll be there soon," I said.

I tucked the water bottle into my tote, slipped my arm through hers, and leaned my head on her shoulder.

Barbara and Phil met us with hugs at the tiny New Bern airport.

"Mom, I'm making meatloaf for dinner, and some fresh broccoli," Barbara said.

"Sounds good," Mom said, and then she was quiet again.

We all went to bed early. I read for a while from *All Creatures Great and Small*. I'd read it at least ten times, and the familiarity and gentleness of the stories about a veterinarian in rural England always soothed me. I also took a Tylenol PM.

The next morning, we had coffee and toast at the table on Barbara's screened porch. The day was bright, and warmer than I had expected. I pointed out the robins and chickadees at the two feeders hanging outside.

"I hate the trip," Mom said, "but I like it once I get here."

"Do we have time for a walk before we go?" I asked Barbara. I needed to work off some of my nervousness.

"A short one," she said.

Mom said, "I'll take a shower."

Barbara and I headed out. We walked by the big houses along the river. Once or twice, Barbara pointed out one of her favorite trees or plants—but mostly, we were quiet, absorbed in our own thoughts.

Diane was out front rearranging baskets of pink and red tulips when we arrived at McCarthy. She waved as we drove into the parking lot, then came over and helped Mom out of the car.

This time, Diane had an empty two-bedroom apartment to show us. It wasn't the exact one Mom would take, but it had the same layout.

"Your couch would look great over there," I said to Mom.

"Do you think the credenza with the TV on it would fit on that wall?" Mom asked.

"We can get measurements and lay everything out on graph paper," Barbara said.

I pointed out how well the kitchen would work for her to get her own breakfast and lunch.

"I don't cook much anymore," Mom said, mostly to Diane.

Diane said she wouldn't need to, since she would have dinner in the dining room.

Mom studied the bedroom and the big walk-in closet. She asked about additional storage space. Diane showed her the closet in the second bedroom and another one outside on the balcony, where she said people usually stored their deck chairs over the winter.

Mom walked across the living room and leaned against the kitchen counter jutting into the dining area.

"I could set the phone and my calendar on this counter," she said. "Yes, I think this could work."

"I just want her to say 'Sign me up,'" I whispered to Barbara.

As we headed back to the office, Diane stopped several times in the hallway to talk with residents. She also told us that her dad had moved in this year.

"Your father lives here at McCarthy?" I asked, making sure Mom heard.

I gave Barbara the thumbs up sign.

"We'll see," she mouthed.

The halls had been quiet when we arrived, but now people were heading toward the elevators to go downstairs.

"There's a trip to the museum today," Diane explained.

When we got back to the first floor, ten or fifteen residents were sitting on the benches outside the dining room or leaning on their walkers, apparently waiting for the bus. It looked like a granny convention—mostly women, lots of gray hair and warm smiles. I spotted Sophie sitting on her walker/chair and said hello, reminding her that we had met a few months earlier. She got up and pushed her walker toward Mom.

"I'm glad to see you back," she said, "Are you going to move in?"

"I'm thinking about it," Mom said.

"Do it—you won't be sorry." Sophie smoothed her bossy tone with a big smile.

Mom laughed.

I wanted to hug them both.

We went to Diane's office and reviewed the apartment layout for what would be Mom's place: Apartment #306. It was the mirror image of the one we had just seen. Her small balcony looked out onto a field across the street. Mom didn't think she would use the balcony much.

"When do we have to decide?" I asked.

Diane said we had three weeks, until April 10th, to make a deposit, or they would go to the next name on the waiting list. The place would be available May 15th.

None of us thought to ask her why it had become vacant.

"Do you have any other questions?" Diane asked.

"I'm curious about the food," Mom said. "Is there a choice for dinner?"

Diane got out the weekly menu and explained how Mom could

choose what she wanted each night from two specials, and that a few standard items were always available.

"Is it good?" Mom asked.

Diane said she could try it out for herself any night. We said we'd think about it, and maybe come for dinner the next day.

As soon as we walked into Barbara's house, Phil asked, "How did it go?"

"It certainly is a nice place," Mom said.

"Pretty much perfect," I said, hoping I wasn't pushing so hard that I'd get resistance.

Barbara started pulling things out of the refrigerator to make lunch.

"Mom, how about a meatloaf sandwich?" Barbara asked.

"Just half a sandwich for me."

"I'll take the other half," I said. "Let's eat on the porch."

Over lunch, I asked Mom what she was thinking about the apartment.

"I think I should take it," she said.

"Me, too!" Barbara and I said in unison.

Mom said she was ready to sign up, but she was concerned about selling her place and moving by May.

"It's too soon," she said.

Barbara said she had to go to Milwaukee for a trial in early June. "I can't get out of it. I'm the only paralegal who's been on the case since it started. The trial could last all month," she said.

I went to the kitchen to get some water. I pictured the calendar in my mind.

"What if you didn't plan to move until July?" I asked, walking back to the porch.

Mom agreed that would be better, reminding us that her place wasn't even on the market. I suggested she could move even before selling her place.

"Can I afford that?" she said.

I asked her if she had talked to Keith at Smith-Barney.

"He told me not to worry," she said. "His wife, Judy, is a realtor. But how will I do the packing? What about movers?"

"Mom, we're going to help you with all of this," Barbara said.

"We're going to take care of everything," I said. "You won't have to do any packing or moving yourself."

"Alright, I guess I'll do it." Mom shrugged.

I jumped up and kissed her. "I really think this is the right decision, Mom."

Barbara got up and headed to the kitchen. "Coffee, anyone?" she called over her shoulder.

The next day was Saturday, and we drove about an hour and a half to Beaufort, North Carolina, a small sailing port with interesting shops. Barbara had made reservations for lunch at a new restaurant there. It was sunny, and the trees were that yellowish shade of green that you only see in early spring. Mom laughed when the waitress called her "young lady." She ordered one of her favorites, soft-shell crab, and we each had a glass of wine.

I wanted to talk more about the move, to make plans, to be sure that Mom was on board—but the day seemed almost magical, and I didn't want to break the spell.

"If I move here, I want to come to this restaurant again," Mom said.

I looked up from my salad and glanced at Barbara, giving her a look that said, "Did she say 'if?'"

Barbara dropped her head toward her plate and reached for her wine glass.

Mom and I caught a plane the next morning. Barbara made us peanut butter-and-honey sandwiches to take along. Thankfully, the trip was uneventful, but it still took most of the day, and by the time we reached the condo, we were both tired. I suggested we order a pizza for dinner. Mom asked me to get out some hummus and crackers to snack on, and to pour some wine.

We settled into our usual seats in the sunroom and watched the news. During the commercials, Mom muted the TV, and I suggested a plan to keep things moving on McCarthy Court.

"How about I change my plane to the afternoon, and we can fill out the paperwork for McCarthy together and get the check in the mail?" I offered.

"I can do it."

I swirled the wine in my glass.

"I know," I said. "I just thought you might like some help."

"I need to think about it for another day or two."

I was too weary to push things any further that night. I took a deep breath and went to get the pizza.

When I got back, Mom was dozing in her chair with the TV on. She woke easily when I came into the room, and insisted on making some salad to go with the pizza. I set up the teak TV trays with plastic Vera placemats and matching napkins.

After dinner, we watched *60 Minutes*. We both hated Andy Rooney's grumpy tirade.

Chapter 8

As soon as I landed at the Miami airport the next day, I called my friend Kate and asked if I could swing by on my way home.

"I need your advice about my mom," I said.

Kate, a nurse with a master's degree in public administration and a doctorate in leadership education, had been written up in the local paper for her work in end-of-life care—but mostly, she was my trusted friend and confidant. When I arrived at her house, she made tea, and we sat at the huge butcher block island in her kitchen, a place where I had cooked and eaten and cried before. I filled her in on the trip to New Bern and my conversation with Mom the night before.

"I'm afraid she's going to back out," I said.

"Mel, I keep telling you, you have to get a professional involved—a doctor, a social worker. Somebody other than you and Barbara to tell her she's going to have to move."

"I keep thinking she'll come around. She's always been so sensible."

"It's way too scary for her."

I took a sip of my tea and added a little more honey.

"Why can't she just trust us?" I moaned.

"It's not about trust. It's about fear. She doesn't want to leave her familiar cocoon, even though she's outgrown—or, more accurately—outlived it."

A few days later, I talked to Mom. I wasn't surprised to hear that she was waffling about McCarthy Court. She listed the same reasons I'd heard before—she didn't really need to be anywhere else; she liked it where she was; it would be too hard to move.

"How will I get to New Bern?" she whined. "And anyway, if I need help, I can hire someone right here in New Port Richey."

I took a deep breath and reached back to pet the cat, who was sharing my office chair and cuddling up against my back.

"Mom, I know this is hard, but honestly, I think it's the best option."

I reiterated that Barbara and I were too far away from New Port Richey, and that we would take care of all the moving. I reminded Mom how perfect McCarthy Court was.

The cat moved, and I edged her onto my lap.

"It isn't going to get any easier to make this move," I said. "You have to be tough. I promise, Barbara and I will make it all as easy as possible."

"I don't know, Mel. I just don't think I can do it."

Please don't make me come over there and take this out of your hands, I thought. In my head, I sounded like a parent warning a misbehaving child with "Don't make me come in there." I had always thought of it as a threat, but now I understood that it was a plea: *Please don't make me be mean. Please be good. Please be my smart, capable mom again.*

"Alright, Mom, but think about it some more. We still have a few days before the payment is due. I really think you'll be happy there."

When I called Mom two days later, she told me she had discussed it with Lenore.

"I decided to do it, even though I'm scared. I sent the check this morning."

Yes! I thought. I punched my left hand into the air to signal a win, and sent a silent word of thanks to Lenore.

"That's great," I said.

"We'll see," she replied.

After I hung up the phone, I stared out my office window at some seagulls dive-bombing the water where my neighbor had tossed out breadcrumbs. I tried to put myself in Mom's place—leaving friends and her home of thirty-five years. I wished I could do the *I Dream of Jeannie* blink and instantly transport Mom and all her belongings from New Port Richey to New Bern. I wished Mom had a pussycat like mine to comfort her.

I let Barbara know that the check was on its way. She said she would call Diane to fill her in. I encouraged her to call Mom in a day or so.

About a week later, Diane called Barbara. The check and paperwork had not arrived.

"Give it another day or two," I said when Barbara called me.

I questioned Mom, and she assured me she had sent everything to Diane—but two more days went by, and nothing had arrived at McCarthy Court. Now we were past the deadline. Barbara told Diane that Mom definitely wanted the apartment, and she agreed to hold it for another week.

"What in the hell?" I said on the phone with Barbara.

"Maybe she got the wrong address."

"Damn. I think I'll have to go over there, figure this out, and get another check in the mail. I'll go this weekend. Damn."

I called Mom, and told her I had just set up a meeting with a colleague at Hospice of the Florida Suncoast for Monday. It was a lie. I told her I'd be coming over on Sunday to spend two nights.

"Oh, good," she said. "I love it when you stay here."

I didn't tell her that the check had not made it to McCarthy Court. I figured I'd deal with it when I got there.

I arrived at Mom's condo around noon. We shared a turkey sandwich and an apple. It had only been a few weeks since our trip to New Bern, but she looked smaller to me.

"Mom, have you lost weight?"

"Maybe. I'm not very hungry these days."

"You have to eat," I said. I decided to make a big pot of lentil soup for dinner. I thought the smell of food might perk up her appetite. I'd freeze the leftovers for her to have during the week.

Mom and I went to Publix together to get the lentils and other things I needed for the soup. I also picked up the ingredients for a beef stew, some frozen Stouffer's Swedish meatballs, and some whole-milk yogurt. I wanted to be sure that Mom had nutritious—even fattening—food around.

Once I'd put the soup together, I joined Mom in the sunroom to watch a movie—*Notting Hill* was on. We'd both seen it before, but the cheerful romance was perfect for the day. As it ended, I pushed the mute button on the remote.

"Mom, we're going to have to send another check to McCarthy Court. The one you sent never arrived."

"What?"

"It never arrived. It must have gotten lost in the mail."

"Oh, Mel, this is so hard. I want to be strong, but there's so much to do. My place isn't even up for sale."

"I know. But I'm here now." I could see that she really needed me to be strong. I told her I would call the bank and cancel the first check. Then we'd send another.

"And I'll call Judy, the real estate agent, about getting the condo on the market. Please try not to worry," I said.

"But what about your meeting?"

"It was cancelled," I lied, then quickly followed with a version of the truth. "Anyway, I really wanted to see you."

We were both ready for our glass of wine. I put out cheese and crackers, and made sure Mom ate some.

The next day, Mom and I sat at the table in the sunroom. I filled out the extra set of papers we had for McCarthy Court, and Mom signed them. I watched her write out the check in her now-wobbly hand-writing. I put everything in the FedEx package I'd prepared using my business account. I wasn't going to let this one get lost.

"Okay, now we need to make some copies," I said.

"We can do it at the condo office," Mom said.

"Perfect," I said. "We can stop there, and then drop off the package on the way to lunch."

Mom folded her hands on the table.

"Melly, I'm sorry to be so much trouble."

"It's okay, Mom. But this is good decision. Really, it is." I took her hand and squeezed it.

I called Keith's wife, Judy. Keith was Mom and Daddy's longtime financial planner, currently with Smith-Barney. Mom always referred to Keith and his partner, Rick, as "the boys," and she thought of them as extended family. Because of Mom and Daddy's special relationship with Keith, I knew Judy would be the right agent to sell Mom's condo. She said there was no rush to get the condo on the market if Mom wasn't going to move until July. She thought we should wait a bit. I asked her to prepare some information on other sales so we could start thinking about price.

Mom and I went out to a local coffee shop for lunch, after making our copies and dropping the package in the FedEx outgoing box. Mom ordered a BLT, and I had a salad. She ate very little, and I did most of the talking. Back at the condo, Mom napped while I made beef stew for dinner.

Over our evening wine and cheese, I talked to Mom about my schedule. I could see how fragile she was, and I wanted to come back soon. I was going to Washington, D.C. for the annual conference of the National Hospice and Palliative Care Organization (NHPCO) in about week. I went every year—and that year, 2007, I was giving two presentations. I told her I would come back to visit her the week after the meeting.

"Are you sure you can do that?" she asked in a way that sounded like a plea.

"Yes, I'm sure," I said. "Now, let's have some stew."

The NHPCO conference was held at the Omni Shoreham, a historic hotel built in 1930. When I was a kid, Mom and Daddy would sometimes go to the hotel's famed Blue Room to see Tom Lehrer, or a jazz quartet. In the early 2000s, the Shoreham was acquired by the Omni chain, but it still had the elegant look and feel of a grand hotel. I studied the hallway displays of menus from celebrity dinners, entertainment programs for the Blue Room, and photos of the clientele.

When I arrived for the meeting, the small garden out front was wall-to-wall blooming tulips surrounding a dogwood tree in full flower. It was a spectacular show. I took a photo on my iPhone to show Mom.

The conference was great. I always looked forward to connecting with colleagues from around the country. Barbara called it "hob-nobbing with my fellow wizards," quoting from *The Wizard of Oz*. Between the beautiful spring weather, my successful presentations, and the fact that Mom was set to go to North Carolina, I was feeling better than I had in weeks—maybe months. The last day of the conference, after the morning plenary session, I found a seat in the lobby and called Mom. I planned to tell her about the flowers and how the Shoreham reminded me of her, all dressed up in her tea-colored lace cocktail dress to go out with Daddy.

"Hi, Mom. How are you doing?"

"Not so good, Mel."

I felt my good mood evaporate and my stomach clench.

"What's wrong?"

"I can't do it, Mel. I can't go to New Bern."

"Mom, I thought we had made this decision."

"I know, but I can't. I really think I'll be all right here."

Right there, in the beautiful lobby of the Shoreham hotel, I was crying. I didn't care if anyone saw me. In fact, I wished someone would come over and offer to help. I needed help, and after all, I was surrounded by all that hospice compassion—but no one seemed to notice.

"Mom, we've already been over this. You need to be nearer to one of us."

"I know, but it's just too hard."

Now she was crying. I couldn't bear it. She sounded so miserable, so scared. I had to help her. There had to be another way.

"Alright," I said. "When I come next week, we'll look at other options—maybe some kind of home care. But let's not cancel McCarthy Court yet. I need some time."

"I'm sorry, Mel."

"It's okay. We'll figure it out. I love you, Mom."

I didn't want to call Barbara until I had a plan. I went up to my room to calm down, and thought about what Kate had said. Mom might listen to a professional—but who? Then I remembered a woman I'd met about a year before, while working on a project for the American Hospice Foundation. She had said she was a geriatric care manager (GCM). I'd never heard the term, so I'd asked her about it. Geriatric care managers (now called aging life care experts) help families find, hire, and manage services for older adults—things like nursing care, homemaking services, even moving. She told me there was an association for certified managers.

I leaned across the hotel bed, picked up my computer, and googled "Geriatric Care Management." I found the association website, and learned that certified GCMs conduct assessments, offer advice about what kinds of services a parent might need, and connect clients with various providers. Using the geographic search function on the website, I found two care managers near New Port Richey, and wrote down their names and contact information.

"I think I screwed up," I said to Barbara. I told her about the call with Mom, and my promise to look into some other arrangement. Then I told her about the GCMs.

"I want to set up an appointment for when I'm there next week. Maybe Mom could stay in New Port Richey."

"I wish," Barbara said, "but I doubt it."

We agreed, though, that it wouldn't hurt to talk to someone.

The first GCM I called worked for an agency, and she was basically a representative selling their home care services. It didn't sound to me like she wanted to—or could—offer any kind of innovative solutions. The second one, Karen, also worked for an agency, but she said she could recommend all kinds of services. She offered a free assessment visit to see what kind of help Mom needed. I set up an appointment for the following week. I couldn't help feeling hopeful.

Karen, Mom, and I sat at the round table in the sunroom. Mom was surprisingly perky, smiling and answering all of Karen's questions in detail. I added a few comments about my concerns—losing weight, less stable on her feet, not going out as much. Karen kept her attention on Mom, asking what she usually had for lunch and for dinner, how often she went out, and what she did all day. It was all very conversational. Karen took notes, but it didn't seem like a test or medical exam.

"You seem to be doing pretty well," Karen said to Mom.

"I think so, even though I am slowing down," Mom replied.

"I guess our main question is about the future," I said. "Mom has the option to move to North Carolina and live in a senior apartment just five minutes from my sister. We want her to do that, but she thinks she wants to stay here." I explained to Karen that McCarthy Court was a typical Adult Congregate Living Facility (ACLF) where residents received dinner along with other minimal services.

Karen said that being near family was always best, if it was an option. I held my breath.

"Where in North Carolina?" Karen asked.

"New Bern," Mom answered.

Karen had been to New Bern. Her brother, a dentist, lived and practiced there. I wondered how this could be true. New Bern had only about 40,000 residents, and this random woman I had found on the Internet not only knew about it, but also had family there? I made a note to get her brother's name. Mom would need a new dentist. This wasn't just coincidence—it was synchronicity. New Bern was meant to be.

Karen asked Mom if there was some reason she didn't want to move.

"It seems so daunting. Packing, selling my condo, all of it," Mom said.

I sipped my water and channeled Kate. I was dying to say something, but I knew I had to let the professional do the work.

"Well, I could help you with packing and moving," Karen said, "and help you find a good real estate agent."

"We have someone," Mom said.

I couldn't stay quiet any longer. I told Karen that Barbara and I were prepared to take care of everything—moving, the condo sale, and getting Mom settled in her new home—but I was grateful to know we could call on her if we needed help.

"So, you really think I should go?" Mom asked Karen.

"I really do," she replied.

I got up and went around the table. I stood behind Mom, wrapping my arms around her shoulders.

She put her hands on my arms, squeezing them. She closed her eyes and sighed deeply.

"Okay," she said. "Okay."

Chapter 9

MOM HAD BEEN RIGHT WHEN SHE'D SAID, "This is hard." I was beginning to understand that even though she had agreed to move to McCarthy Court, she would never be enthusiastic about it, and would probably want to back out again at some point. Barbara and I would have to hold the line. I couldn't be weak. I couldn't waver.

I also realized that we had to get the wheels in motion. Barbara and I agreed that I'd take charge of all the things that had to happen in New Port Richey—planning the move, hiring the movers, and getting Mom's condo sold, or at least on the market. Then I would pass the baton, and Barbara would take over in New Bern.

"Right now, there's way more to do here than there," I said, "but considering how long she may live in New Bern, you'll be getting the lion's share of the work."

I promised her I'd visit often, and help in every way I could.

"Mel, it's okay."

It was late April of 2007, and the move was planned for July. Given how much there was to do and how little of it Mom seemed able to do on her own, I could see that I would need to spend a lot of time with her. My consulting workload was relatively low at the time, and I had a colleague—another consultant—who would back me up. I was worried about being away from Klein, but when I talked with him, he said I should do whatever I needed to. *God love him!* I thought.

From late April to early July, I split my time between Miami and New Port Richey. I visited for three or four days out of every ten, spacing my trips so Mom wouldn't be alone to brood and worry more than a few days in a row.

Every time I left to go back to Miami, I fretted about how she would get along without me there to keep her fed and moving. Usually, I coordinated with Lenore to be sure she could visit, and maybe take Mom to dinner one of the days I was gone. I also let the condo office staff know when I was coming and going. They were like her local family, and would call some mornings and urge her to stop by the office for coffee and a chat.

On every trip, I tried to get a few things done to prepare for the move. We met with Keith at Smith-Barney about finances. Keith's wife, Judy, came over with all the paperwork to get the condo on the market. Mom's depression and anxiety made her tired. She could only handle one meeting a day, and even though she had made it clear that she wanted me to be in charge, she and I both wanted her to stay involved.

One of our "chores" was to decide which furniture she would take to McCarthy Court, and what we would sell or give away. Barbara had measured the new apartment, and I drew out the rooms on graph paper and made scaled cutouts of Mom's furniture so we could see how things fit.

Mom seemed to enjoy trying out different furniture arrangements on the graph paper drawing. She'd always had a knack for decorating, and strong opinions about how things should look. When I bought my first house, I told her I wanted curtains with an abstract print for my bedroom. She said, "No, you don't. You need a solid color in there." She was right.

When we had a final list of what would go to her new home, I set up appointments with two movers. The first one went well—the representative was a nice guy, and I was silently grateful that he kept including Mom in the conversation rather than just addressing me. Mom was animated while he was there, then collapsed in exhaustion as soon as he left. Later that day, I asked her what she thought.

"It sounds like they can handle the move," she said.

"I have another mover coming tomorrow, so we can compare."

"Really? Can't we just go with this one? I think the price is fine."

I cancelled the other meeting. I could see she'd had enough.

The days together were slow and emotionally charged. We both woke up early, having turned in early the night before. Mom fixed her coffee, and I made sure she took her antidepressant and antianxiety medications. She was shaky until they kicked in, but she worked on the Jumble puzzle in the newspaper and read the comics. I went jogging, then we took showers, dressed, and went out to do errands.

Usually, I let Mom drive. I figured it gave her some measure of control, and I wanted to make sure she was still able to manage the car. I was worried about her navigating the unfamiliar streets of New Bern—even though she would not be driving far—but Mom was determined to take her ten-year-old Nissan Altima with her to North Carolina.

After I fixed lunch and made sure Mom ate, she usually napped in Daddy's chair. I did some work or made to-do lists: clean out the safe deposit box at the bank, wrap and ship the most fragile and precious items that we didn't want to trust to the movers, follow up on condo-sale paperwork. Shortly after five, we settled in for wine and cheese, then dinner in front of the TV. I made grilled cheese sandwiches, chicken soup, and meatloaf with baked potatoes, comfort foods to soothe us both as we faced an unwelcome future.

One morning, when I got up and went into Mom's room, I found her sitting on the edge of the bed in the dark. The sheets were tangled around her legs, and she was crying. I sat next to her and wrapped her in a hug.

"I didn't want to wake up," she sobbed, "I wish I'd just died in the night, so I wouldn't have to move."

My heart was breaking. I could feel her anguish, and I knew I had to be the strong one. I closed my eyes and retreated into cold rationality. It felt awful.

"I know it's hard, Mom. But it will be okay. I promise." Did I know it would be alright? I didn't, but I knew we had to do something, and this was the best option.

We sat for a few more minutes, and I held her tight until she raised her head and reached for a tissue. She blew her nose as I gently untangled the sheet and blanket.

"Come on," I said, "Let's get some coffee and toast." *And an extra Xanax,* I thought.

Mom stood up and shuffled into the bathroom.

Later that day, I hid in the walk-in closet in the guest room and called Barbara. I didn't want Mom to hear our conversation.

"She said she'd rather die than move," I whispered. "I feel like the meanest mommy ever, making her do this 'for her own good.'"

"You're doing great, Mel."

"Well, it doesn't feel great."

"Why don't you get out for a while? Go to the mall or something."

"Yeah, maybe."

Mom was napping in the sunroom, so I left her a note and went to Starbucks. I ordered my usual decaf cappuccino, and added an oatmeal raisin cookie. I deserved it. I sat on a bench in the shopping mall and watched people walk by—teenagers in laughing groups, and older women, some with walkers and some leaning on the arm of an even older-looking man.

It's the circle of life, I thought. *But right now, it feels more like the tilt-a whirl than the merry-go-round.*

One bright spot was that the sale of Mom's condo went surprisingly smoothly. A neighbor who lived just two doors away wanted to buy it, because Mom's end unit offered more light and a second outdoor terrace. His offer was below market value, but after a few weeks, we decided to accept it.

"I feel better knowing I'll have that money in the bank," Mom said.

Anything that made her feel better was fine by me.

Over the weeks of my frequent visits, Mom's driving went from passable to scary. She went too slowly, or sped up at the wrong time. She barely had the strength to turn the steering wheel of the front-wheel-drive Altima. After she hit a boat trailer parked in front of the house across the street from her condo, she admitted it was hard to twist around when she needed to back up.

"But I hardly ever have to back up," she told me. "I always park where I can pull through to head it facing forward."

A few months before, I had made a halfhearted attempt to discuss it with her.

"Mom, are you alright driving?"

She reiterated what she'd told Barbara more than a year earlier. "Well, I don't drive at night anymore. I never go far, and only to places I know—Publix, the hairdresser, or to see friends."

What did I expect her to say? How would she get around without a car? Maybe some kind of senior car service? It made me tired just to think about it.

Then, one day in June, I had to grab the strap above the passenger window as she swung into the parking lot of Dean's Hair Boutique. She made a wide arc at about forty miles per hour, barely braking, and narrowly missing the palm-fronded fruit stand. It was time.

In a way, the move was the perfect opportunity. All I had to do was convince her not to take the car—but her ongoing depression unnerved me. With this move, Mom was giving up her home, and much of her independence. I couldn't take driving away from her, too. It had to be about the car, and not about driving. And somehow, it had to be her decision.

We'd made a plan for getting the car to New Bern. Barbara and her husband Phil would fly down to Tampa, and Phil would drive the car back to North Carolina while Mom and Barbara flew up.

I appealed to Mom's strong desire not to be a burden.

"Hey, Mom. You know how much Phil hates to fly. Wouldn't it be better to sell the car?" I asked.

"But how will I get around in New Bern? I can't ask Barbara to drive me everywhere."

"McCarthy Court has the courtesy van. You won't need your car."

"What if I just want to go out for a sandwich?"

Knowing I was lying, I told her she could buy a new car if she needed one.

"Why buy a new one? I have a good car," she said.

Once again, I escaped to Starbucks to console myself. I found a comfortable chair and called Kate.

"I feel like I have to be so tough with Mom. It's painful for both of us."

"This is never easy," Kate said. "Nobody does this without heartache."

I sipped my cappuccino.

"Why can't I figure out how to make things better for her?"

"I keep telling you that you have to get somebody like a social worker to take the heat for things like not driving anymore. Set it up so you can be the supportive daughter."

It was great advice, but how I would do it, I had no idea.

Mom was scheduled to go to the doctor during my next visit. I thought it might be time to increase her antidepressant medication, and I wanted to ask Dr. G. if she could take more Xanax when she needed it.

I went with Mom to the doctor, just as she had so often accompanied me to the pediatrician. Now, I sat in the parent chair while Dr. G. checked her blood pressure. He focused all his attention on her, barely acknowledging my presence.

"So, how are you doing?" Dr. G. asked.

"I'm alright," Mom answered, "but I think this will be my last visit with you. I'm moving to North Carolina."

Dr. G. nodded as Mom continued. "I'm scared. I'm too old to start over in a new place."

I winced.

I said, "I'm concerned about how her hands shake, particularly in the morning."

Dr. G. looked straight at Mom. "What do you think?" he asked her. "Probably just feeling nervous, right?"

She nodded.

He suggested increasing her antidepressant, and said she could take an extra half-dose of Xanax if she was particularly anxious, but not if she was going to be driving.

Driving! The car! Suddenly I picked up the cue. *Dr. G. is a professional,* I thought. *Maybe he can help.*

I tucked my hands under my legs to help me stay still. "I have a question," I said. "Do you have any opinions on when it's time to stop driving?" Dr. G. looked at me for a second, then sat forward in his chair, his knees almost touching Mom's.

"I tell my patients that their families are the people who love them and care about them the most. If your family is concerned about your driving, you should listen to them," he said. "I ask my patients to think about how they would feel if they were driving and someone got hurt."

"I would feel awful," Mom said. "Maybe I shouldn't take the car to North Carolina after all."

I concentrated on my breathing, and tried to channel my yoga teacher.

Dr. G. continued, "If your family is worried, but you think you can drive perfectly well, go to the driver's license bureau and take a test. If you pass, then you're okay to drive, and your family will know it."

"No, no," Mom said, "I think we should go ahead and sell the car."

Dr. G. patted her knee. I wanted to hug him, but I kept sitting on my hands and spoke quietly, the way I did in business meetings when the client started to think that my idea was his own.

"You know, Mom, I think that's a good idea."

In my mind, I was already composing the ad for the *Auto Trader*.

Chapter 10

I SPENT HOURS, often between midnight and 3 A.M., thinking about how to protect Mom from the trauma of watching as her home was disassembled. The move was scheduled for July 9th—a Monday. As the plan took shape, I was like a stage manager, and I wanted my play, *Mom's Move*, to go off without a hitch. I told Barbara we should travel to New Port Richey a couple of days early, and do very little packing—just the clothes, fragile items, and valuables that would go with her and Mom on the plane to New Bern. I scheduled the car service that would take the two of them to the airport for 8:30 A.M., and the moving van for 9:00 A.M., so Mom wouldn't even see the packing boxes. I'd stay behind, supervise the movers, and finish cleaning out the condo. Mom would stay at Barbara and Phil's house for the five days it would take the movers to drive to New Bern.

I made lists—a list of the furniture, kitchenware, linens, and decorative items that were going to North Carolina, and a list of those that were staying behind; a list of phone numbers for the United Van Lines contact in Florida, the contact in North Carolina, and the company that was handling the closing on the condo sale; a list of Mom's medications; and a list of the most important and hard-to-replace legal and insurance papers. I made copies of the lists for Barbara.

I packed the critical papers in a zipped tote bag that Barbara would carry on the plane. I refilled Mom's prescriptions, to be sure she wouldn't run out before they could be transferred to a pharmacy in New Bern.

I took pictures of the living room in Florida, and sent them to Barbara to help her recreate the look in the new apartment at McCarthy Court. One item was crucial: Mom's glass-shelved étagère. She loved it, and often took me on a "tour" of the contents—family heirlooms like the eighteen-inch bisque shepherd and shepherdess figurines that had belonged to her grandmother; a few decorative plates, including one that featured a huge dead duck; and a hodgepodge collection of bird figurines. I thought that having it set up just right would go a long way toward making her new apartment feel like home.

The first act of my play went pretty well. I drove over from Miami knowing I would need the SUV to take things back to my house, and picked up Barbara at the Tampa airport. We arrived at the condo just after noon on the Saturday before the move. Mom pulled out some sliced turkey and ham. We made sandwiches, and took them to the table in the sunroom.

"Barb, did Mel tell you about the party the condo office had for me?" asked Mom. She continued without waiting for Barbara's reply. "We had pizza. The whole maintenance crew

Mom's étagère. I took this photo of the étagère before Mom moved out of the New Port Richey condo, and used it to recreate the tableau each time she moved.

and some of the security guards came, plus everyone from the front office," she said. "And they're going to plant a tree in my honor—right next to Clubhouse 2."

Barbara said, "I think they're going to miss you."

"I'll definitely miss them," said Mom. She grabbed a tissue and blew her nose. "I'm sorry," she said, "I can't help it."

"It's okay," I said. I got up and gave her a hug.

"I'm so glad you girls are here." Mom reached out and grabbed Barbara's hand.

Barbara offered to make coffee, but Mom said she would do it. She took another tissue, wiped her nose, and headed for the kitchen. Barbara picked up the plates and followed her. I stared out at the canal, and wondered if it was too soon to have a glass of wine.

As we sipped our coffee, Mom asked what the plans were. I downplayed the need to do anything. I said Barbara and I might pack a few things, and that I hoped we could all go out to dinner.

While Mom and Barbara took the coffee mugs to the dishwasher, I looked into the storage closet off the sunroom. The two-drawer metal filing cabinet and the fireproof lockbox sat on the floor on the left side. Mom and I had been through them both, and pulled out the critical papers. Daddy's old steamer trunk was on the right side. He had used it when he was a teenager to ship his things from home in Philadelphia to boarding school in Vermont. When we were kids, it had been tucked into a basement storeroom, packed with clothes that were out of season or waiting to be handed down from Barbara to me. Now it held decorations that Mom pulled out for various holidays—fragile pastel-painted eggs, each carefully wrapped in tissue; two small, colorful Easter baskets; papier mâché pumpkins and some dried, multicolored corn cobs; an artificial Christmas wreath decorated with dried flowers; and the wooden figurine of the *Nutcracker* Prince Mom had bought at intermission when we went to see the Christmas ballet.

I decided to inventory the four-drawer oak bureau at the back of the closet, since it would not be going to New Bern, and its contents would have to be packed. The top two drawers held several expanding files. Some were filled with greeting cards and letters to Mom and Daddy from Barbara and me. The others held clippings and notes for her columns for *The Comet*. The bottom drawers were filled with packing materials, like bubble wrap and tape, along with multicolored wrapping paper and rolls of ribbon. I pulled everything out so I could see it all, wrap anything fragile, and repack it to be shipped safely.

Just then, Barbara and Mom walked back into the sunroom.

"Hey Barb," I said, "How about we pack everything from this bureau into the trunk?"

Barbara stepped into the closet, and Mom headed for her chair.

After a few minutes, Mom said, "I hate this. I really hate this."

I looked up from the bubble wrap, ashamed that I'd forgotten my well-laid plans.

"I know," I said. "I'm sorry. We don't need to do this now." I turned off the light and slid the pocket door to the closet closed.

Barbara said, "Let's watch a movie."

Mom asked if we had seen *You've Got Mail*, and we had, but agreed to see it again. Nothing like watching beautiful people struggle toward a happy ending to take you out of your own troubles. Mom napped in her chair.

The next day was Sunday. The three of us sat at the rattan table reading the paper, drinking coffee, and picking at some fruit and toast. Barbara offered to help Mom choose clothes for the trip, and once they headed for the bedroom, I snuck into the storage closet to finish the packing I had started the day before.

Act II of *Mom's Move* was proving to be a downer. Why had we come so early? There was nothing to do except worry. We worked on the Sunday crossword puzzle together. After lunch, Mom napped, and Barbara and I very quietly packed up some of the more fragile knick-knacks from the étagère, hoping Mom wouldn't notice.

Finally, it was time for cocktails. We toasted to Mom's last night in the condo. She didn't smile.

"Try to remember how nice New Bern is," I said.

"I just can't believe it," Mom said. "I can't believe I'm leaving my home."

Then, she cried.

At bedtime, I urged her to take an extra half a Xanax. I took the other half.

On Monday, moving day, we all woke up early. At 5 A.M., I lay in bed and listened as Mom went into the kitchen. *Time for Act III*, I thought.

"Are you awake?" Barbara asked.

"Yeah." I rolled over to face her in the other bed.

"Are you ready?" she said.

"No."

I went into the kitchen, hugged Mom from behind, and snuggled my head between her shoulder and neck. I thought about all the times she had gotten me through when I was scared—new schools, overnight Girl Scout camping, my first date with a boy.

"You doing okay?" I asked.

"Okay," she said.

We had coffee, took showers, and got dressed. I cleaned up the kitchen, and carefully set aside one mug for me to use after the movers were gone. Barbara helped Mom pack her toothbrush and face cream in the ancient plastic blue-flowered zipper case she took on every trip. All the luggage was lined up at the front door by 8 A.M., and we sat down for a second cup of coffee before the car service arrived at 8:30.

The mood was somber but peaceful. I was so pleased that we hadn't torn Mom's home apart with her in it.

And then I saw the moving van. They were forty-five minutes early. I ran out the front door and accosted the driver as he got out of the truck.

"You cannot come in," I said. "I specifically scheduled the move for 9 A.M. so that my mother would be gone. She's still here."

"We're a little ahead of schedule," he said, "We won't take anything out. We'll just start packing."

"Do you have to?" I asked, "Please, please wait ten minutes, just until the car comes to take her to the airport."

He explained that it would take them a few minutes to get the boxes and packing paper out of the truck, but then they wanted to get started. I told him to start in the bedroom, figuring Mom wouldn't need to go back in there.

I was shaking as I walked back to the condo.

"What happened?" Barbara asked.

"They're early," I answered. "Best-laid plans and all that. I tried to stall them."

Barbara said she'd keep Mom in the sunroom.

The car service arrived a little past 8:30, while the movers were still staging outside.

Mom, Barbara, and I followed as the driver took the luggage to the car. I wrapped Mom in a hug.

"I love you," I said. "I'll see you soon."

"Okay," she said.

Barbara helped Mom into the back seat of the car, then got in on the other side. I watched until they were out of sight.

The rest of that day went by quickly. The movers packed everything from the kitchen, the bathrooms, Mom's room, and the storage closets. I monitored them closely, even though we had placed labels—*stay* or *go*—on every piece of furniture, and almost every shelf. Barbara called at around 3:00 to let me know they had landed in New Bern. Their connecting flight had been delayed.

"Mom was a real trouper." I knew she was making it sound better than it was. I had traveled with Mom.

The movers finished up around four in the afternoon. I went through the checklist of everything they had in the truck, and signed the papers.

Standing in the middle of the now-empty living room, I could see the well-traveled pathways on the rug. For the first time, I noticed how much furniture was left to deal with. I walked through every room, taking a quick inventory. The guest room beds and dresser, which I would use for the next few days, were going to one of the condo maintenance workers. I decided to give them the sheets and blankets, too, and made a note to leave time to launder them before I left. Mom's "good" china and silverware were on the truck to New Bern, and would end up at Barbara's house. Other than that, the dining room had been left intact. I planned to pack up my grandmother's china and some of Mom's glassware to take to my house. That left the books, a few bottles of wine, lots of small serving and decorative pieces, and the beautiful Scandinavian teak furniture—a six-foot oval table plus two leaves, six chairs, and a large sideboard with a glass-front hutch.

I wandered into the kitchen and realized that most of the food was still there to be sorted through and tossed, donated, or taken to my house. I checked the liquor cabinet, and was delighted to find that the movers had not packed any of it. I pulled a serving of the homemade beef stew I had made for Mom out of the freezer, then remembered there was no microwave—nor were there pans to heat it up in. Searching for anything that might work, I found the broiler pan in a drawer under the oven. Mom had used it to make gravy, so I knew it could sit on top of the stove. I put the partially thawed stew in the pan on low heat, fixed myself a Manhattan in the one remaining mug, and headed for the sunroom.

The rattan furniture remained where it had been since Mom and Daddy had moved in thirty-three years earlier. Now I sat in Mom's chair, formerly Daddy's chair. The teak TV tables were gone, and so was the TV. I stared at the blank, silent wall and cried.

I ate dinner at the sunroom table, looking out at the canal and reading leftover sections of the Sunday newspaper. I called Klein, and told him I was too tired to talk. I took a long, hot shower and got into bed with *All Things Wise and Wonderful*, one of the James Herriot books from Mom's shelf. I opened it to the middle, read maybe two pages, and fell asleep.

Despite all the preliminary sorting and cleaning we had done, it took me two full days to pack the boxes bound for my house, tote things to Goodwill, sell the car, and find homes for the left-behind furniture. Over the years, Mom had done a great job pruning and organizing, or I would have been there for a week or more. The fact that she had been diligent about getting rid of broken and unwanted items meant that Mom really cared about everything that was left. I struggled with every decision. Well, maybe not every one. It was easy to throw away old cleaning supplies, some threadbare washcloths, and the ancient forty-pound ironing board that Mom had owned since she was married.

The truth is, I made it harder than it needed to be. The new owners had said I could leave anything I didn't want, and I could have called one of those estate sale companies and sold them everything for one price—but I was afraid I might miss something I should keep. By the end of day one, I felt too paralyzed to make any more decisions. When I realized I'd been staring at the books in the dining room for fifteen minutes trying to figure out what to do, I called Lenore, and asked her to come and help me.

Early the next morning, Lenore identified a few books that she thought might be valuable, and said I should have them appraised. She told me to choose five that I really wanted; I settled for ten. She chose five that she wanted. Then she helped me pack what was left, and she took them to donate to the library. We did the same thing with the porcelain and glass collectibles in the dining room sideboard. We each chose items we really wanted, then packed the rest for Lenore's church bazaar.

That left the car and the furniture to deal with. A good friend from Suncoast Hospice, where I still did some work now and then, came to my rescue. Her daughter-in-law bought the car, and her work colleague took the dining room furniture. I had the car cleaned and detailed, and drove it to my friend's house that evening. We went out for dinner, and then she drove me back to the condo.

I poured some wine into a paper cup I'd found in a drawer, picked up one of my ten books, and headed for the sunroom. I sipped my wine and looked at the room where Mom and Daddy had spent most of their time—the room where Daddy had died. I couldn't imagine that furniture anywhere else. I decided to leave it—my version of a shrine, perhaps.

The next morning, I made myself some instant coffee. I carried it to the sunroom and sat at the rattan table looking out at the canal. A single pelican sat on the edge of the sea wall. The tide flowed slowly toward the gulf. Every few minutes, a mullet burst through the surface, twisting slightly and then flopping back into the water. Daddy once asked me why mullet jump. I pretended to know all about it, telling him it was an evolutionary holdover from a time when they leapt from pool to pool looking for food. At first, he seemed to believe the story; then we both laughed. I missed him, and at the same time, I was grateful for the sudden death that had spared him the anguish of further aging.

I wandered outside and dumped the last of my coffee in the canal. Then I got into my overstuffed SUV and drove away from the condo for the last time.

Everything about that move was sad and full of fear. There had been no sense of adventure or new horizons, no excitement about setting up a new household or meeting new people. It represented the end of Mom's complete independence, and it was the end of Barbara's independence from Mom, as well.

During the five days she stayed at Barbara and Phil's house, waiting for her furniture to arrive in New Bern, Mom was miserable, and Barbara had to deal with that misery in close quarters. It was the worst possible time for them to be thrown together without me as a buffer.

Chapter 11

I CALLED BARBARA'S HOUSE EVERY DAY. Mom cried. She begged us to undo everything and let her go back to New Port Richey. I told her to hang in there until the furniture arrived, and she could actually be in her own place.

"Give it a chance," I said. "Give it a month or two, at least."

Barbara said Mom seemed terminally homesick.

"Well, it's only been a few days," I said.

I reminded Barbara about her first week of college. Mom, Daddy, and I had come home from church on Sunday to find Barbara sitting on the living room couch when she was supposed to be on campus.

"Your point?" she asked.

"Mom and Daddy made you go back that very day, saying you had to try it for another few weeks before throwing in the towel. After that, we had to beg you to come home."

"I know, but I was a kid," Barbara whined.

"Well, she probably feels like a kid," I said. "Look, I know it's hard on both of you. But it just has to get better."

When the truck arrived, Barbara and Phil placed the furniture, unpacked the kitchen, made up the bed, and finally brought Mom to McCarthy Court. I was working at the offices of the National Hospice and Palliative Care Organization in Alexandria, Virginia when I got a frantic call from Barbara. Mom wanted her bedsheets—where were they? Mom had used the same sheets for almost a decade. How they had lasted through frequent washings for that long, I cannot imagine. The sheets featured black Japanese-ink-style drawings of a cat on a light brown background, but what Mom really loved was how soft they were.

"I left those sheets for Colleen—you know, the maintenance worker who is taking the bed. They're ancient, and they won't fit her new smaller bed," I told Barbara. Now I was frantic and crying. I'd been trying so hard, and still I was failing Mom.

"Is there any way to get them?"

"I'll try," I said.

I called Susan in the condo office and asked her to help. I told her where the sheets were in the house, and asked if she would mail them to Barbara.

"Of course," Susan said. Then she asked how Mom was doing.

"She's having a hard time, but I keep hoping that once she gets settled, it'll be better. Please call me and let me know if you find the sheets," I said. "I know it sounds crazy, but she really wants them."

Susan called an hour later, and said the sheets were in the mail. I called Barbara.

"Mel, I'm losing it," she said. "My anxiety is out of control. I don't think I can do this. It feels like when I had that breakdown. She's so needy, and I don't know what to do."

"I know. Remember all the times I called you when I was losing it?"

"You're so much better with her than I am." Barbara's voice cracked.

"It's hard for me, too. I've just been around her more. Maybe I should come up there."

"You can't, can you? Don't you have to work?"

"Yes, but so do you," I said.

"I took two days off—told them I was sick. Truly, I am," she said.

"Look, I could reroute my trip back to Florida and come to New Bern for a few days." It was a pain, and I wished I didn't have to, but I knew I'd feel better if I made the trip. I hoped Mom and Barb might feel better, too.

"I'm coming," I said. "I'll be there day after tomorrow."

I flew to Raleigh-Durham and drove the two and a half hours down Route 70 to New Bern. I would come to know this highway well—the Bojangles billboards (Carolina Born and Breaded); Jones Sausage Road; signs for the Nahunta Pork Center; and Wilber's Barbeque. I measured my progress by the larger towns—Clayton, Goldsboro, Kinston—and the final stretch of divided, limited-access road, where the speed limit finally rose from forty-five or fifty to sixty-five miles per hour.

I turned onto the pine straw in Barb and Phil's driveway that afternoon, and at 5:30, we picked up Mom and went out for fish and chips at Captain Ratty's. Mom didn't eat much—some clam chowder, a little salad, and a glass of wine. I asked a lot of questions, and generally tried to keep the conversation upbeat. By 7:00, we were back at McCarthy Court. Mom said she was tired, so I just walked her up to her apartment and said goodnight.

"See you in the morning," I said, "around eight o' clock. Is that okay?"

"Anytime," said Mom.

"Love you," I said as we hugged.

The next day, Barbara and I were up early, as usual, and went for a walk while it was still cool. After a shower, I headed to Harris Teeter, the local grocery store, for a cappuccino and two muffins—one for me, and one for Mom.

Just before 8:00 A.M., I knocked, then pushed open Mom's unlocked door. The furniture—sofa, chairs, heavy marble coffee table, entertainment center and TV—fit the space well. Everything was familiar except the smell—that very specific mixture of Daddy's pipe tobacco, a hint of flowery potpourri, and delicious cooking aromas was missing. Instead, I detected the scent of fresh paint and carpet cleaner. The twenty-year-old furniture looked new, because in Florida, the living room had gotten little use. Now, it was the only furniture outside of the bedrooms. I could see that Mom had chosen one of the floral side chairs as her "throne," and kept one of the teak TV trays nearby. Barbara and Phil had hung some of the artwork, but more of it was stacked near the sliding doors to the balcony. A few unpacked boxes sat next to the kitchen.

"I got tired of setting up," Mom said, "and I could tell Barb was exhausted, so I told her we'd finish another time."

"Well, that's one reason I came, so I could help you get settled. I think we need to set up your étagère and get some plants. Then you'll feel more at home."

"Alright, but not now. Let's just sit and visit."

Sit and visit? I thought. *I want to get to work. I want to get this done. I want you to perk up and get with the program.*

"I brought muffins." I forced my sunniest smile as I pulled them out of the bag and cut each one in half. "Let's share. Do you need a warm-up on your coffee?"

We sat at the card table that temporarily served as her dining area and makeshift desk. I leafed through her mail, and made small talk about the dinner menu for the following week. Mom had to indicate her choices for each evening. She explained that in addition to the two choices each night, you could ask for fried fish or a plain chicken breast. Her favorite so far was the lasagna, and she was eager to try the smothered pork chops. She told me again how much she missed the condo and all her friends.

"Hang in there," I said.

She took a tissue and wiped her eyes.

"Show me around the apartment, and let's see what needs to be done." I stuffed the remainder of the muffins back into the bag and brushed the crumbs off the table and into my hand.

Mom said the bedroom was all set up, and I was amazed how much it looked the one in Florida, except with a smaller bed.

"I need a lighter bedspread," she said. "That one is too heavy for me now, and I like to make the bed every day."

I made a mental note, *new bedspread.*

"Do you need any new clothes?" I asked.

"Not now, but one of my shoes got lost in the move. They were my favorite sandals."

I took the one remaining blue suede Clark sandal, thinking maybe I could find another pair online.

"The guest room needs fixing up," Mom said, and I could see she was right. The closet held unopened boxes, and the single bed needed linens. I got a notepad from the kitchen and started making a list. Mom said she couldn't find the key to the lockbox, so I added "look for key" to my chores.

"Do you need any soap or shampoo?" I asked.

"I don't think so."

I made a note to check the shower and both bathrooms.

"That's it," Mom said. "You've seen the living room and kitchen."

"Well, I guess I'll open a few boxes and put some things away," I said, "Maybe I can get those two boxes out of the dining area."

"Do you have to do that now? I'd rather just watch some TV— maybe a movie."

I could see that she felt overwhelmed and depressed. I was dying to get her place fully set up and organized, hoping it would help her feel better, but I didn't want to push her too hard.

I turned on the TV and found Turner Classic Movies. We watched Katharine Hepburn and Cary Grant in *Bringing Up Baby* for about twenty minutes, until I saw Mom nodding off.

"Why don't you take a little nap?" I said. "And then we can go out to lunch and buy a new bedspread."

She walked back to the bedroom, and soon I heard light snoring.

I closed her bedroom door, and while she slept, I quietly unpacked and set up the étagère, referring to the photos I had taken in Florida.

Over the next two days, between Barbara and me and Mom, we replaced the sandal that had gotten lost in the move (thank you, Zappos), found a place that could re-key the lock box (and then found the missing keys inside—oops), hung up all of Mom's artwork, and set up the guest room. Now she was completely moved in.

On my last day, I stayed for dinner at McCarthy Court. Mom was at a table with Sophie, whose apartment was right across the hall, and four other women. There were men living at McCarthy Court, but they were outnumbered at least ten to one by the women. Christine, the waitress, referred to everyone in the Southern tradition: "Miss Sophie," or "Miss Eleanor." She called me "Sugar."

Sophie drove the conversation. While I could see how she might get annoying, I welcomed her energy. Mom ate well, and spoke to everyone at the table. Could she be feeling better?

Meanwhile, Barbara had had some time off from being with Mom.

"Thanks for coming," Barbara said, as I packed up to leave.

"I wish I could stay." I really wished I could. I knew intellectually that neither Barbara nor I could "make" Mom happy, but I felt like my being there made things better.

"I'll come back soon," I said, "and if it just gets to be too much, we can try to find another option."

"There is no other option."

She was right. We had agreed to this arrangement, and we both knew it wasn't fair to Barbara and Phil.

I called Mom the next day, and the next, and not much had changed—but after about a week, she seemed better. She said Sophie had talked her into going to the social hour—coffee and dough-nuts—in the rec room.

"The coffee wasn't very good, but I met a woman who is in a book club, so I'm going to that next week," Mom said.

"What's the book?" I asked.

"*The Kite Runner*. We read that for my book club in Florida, but I don't mind talking about it again."

Each day, Mom seemed a little more animated. Barbara stopped her daily visits. And then, suddenly, about three weeks after Mom moved in, she started talking about McCarthy Court as if it were the best place ever.

"I just wish I had moved here sooner," she said. "The people are so nice, and there is something fun to do almost every day, if I want to. On Thursday, we're going to the art museum."

I called Barbara.

"Can you believe it?" I asked.

"I know," she said. "It's astonishing. She pretty much never calls me."

"Thank goodness. I was so worried about both of you."

"Me too!"

Once Mom started adjusting to her new surroundings, Barbara introduced her to Dr. S., the primary care physician she and Phil saw. Dr. S. had experience with geriatric patients, and Mom loved him. Since Mom's health was good, she had no need of any specialist doctors.

For nearly one full year, Mom was as happy and as busy as she wanted to be. She and Sophie became good friends. At least twice a week, Mom boarded the minibus with a group of other residents and went off to lunch, shopping, a movie, or a field trip to see the local sights. Barbara brought her over to the house for dinner about once a week. When Mom and I talked, she described the meal in detail, and praised Barbara's cooking.

I called every few days, and visited every three months. In October, I came for Barbara's birthday. In January, I came for Mom's birthday. In April, I came for the azaleas. I always asked Barbara what else I could be doing.

"Honestly, it's not that much trouble," Barbara said. "I do her laundry, and occasionally drive her to the grocery store. Once a month, I take her to Hamp at Trent Hair Designs for a haircut, and we go out for lunch."

As the year passed, we all got comfortable with the new normal. Barbara took over more of Mom's bill-paying, and I worked with Keith (from Smith Barney) and the accountant to make sure Mom's taxes were filed. And Mom seemed just fine with it all.

Then, about a week before my planned visit in July, Mom fell. It was a Wednesday afternoon, and Sophie was playing piano in the recreation room. Mom's rubber-soled sandals, the ones that worked so well to prevent falls on slippery surfaces, caught on the carpet and stopped her forward motion abruptly. As she fell, her right arm grazed the corner of the piano stool, ripping a V-shaped gash from mid-forearm to elbow.

I could imagine the scene—Mom on the floor, looking confused, saying, "I'm okay. I'm okay," as the blood poured from her arm; the others crowding around her; and Sophie, who didn't walk very well, yelling orders.

"Someone get a towel! Pull the emergency cord! Go get Diane from the office."

Barbara called me from the hospital. Mom was in the operating room, where a surgeon was closing her wound, and she would be admitted for a day or so.

After the initial jolt of nerves, I was relieved. She hadn't broken anything. That was what we'd been warned about—a broken hip or shoulder can be the beginning of the end for an older person. I thought Mom would be upset, but Barbara assured me she was not.

"She swears it doesn't hurt," Barbara said, "but I tell you, it looks like her arm was almost ripped off."

Living almost a thousand miles away and getting my information secondhand from Barbara, I was able to preserve a certain view of Mom—as a ninety-two-year-old with no discernable medical problems. If I had seen the medical records back then, I would not have read them with my professional eye. Instead, as the loving and hopeful daughter, I would have focused on the fact that the "review of systems" was "acutely negative," meaning nothing was wrong with her except that horrible gash. I would not have wondered why all those layers of her skin tore so easily, or why she hadn't been able to stop herself from falling, or use her hands to brace as she fell.

Reviewing the same medical records as I write this now, I see what I would have missed. Her wound was a "complex laceration" requiring "debridement," or removal of dead tissue, prior to sewing it up—which meant that overly fragile blood vessels had frayed and robbed the tissue of oxygen. Mom would spend several days in the hospital, and would lose strength every day she was in bed; and she would require physical therapy to restore both strength and balance when she returned home.

Back then, firmly in denial and with my professional antennae at half-mast, I did not see how this fall signaled the beginning of a steeper downward slide.

Chapter 12

I ARRIVED IN NEW BERN FOR MY JULY 2008 quarterly visit just a few days after Mom had been discharged from the hospital and returned to her apartment at McCarthy Court. Except for the huge bandage encircling her arm, she looked much as I had left her three months earlier. Barbara unwound the gauze and followed written instructions for changing the dressing. Once it was exposed, I gasped at the extent of the injury. It was *Frankenstein*-ian—the row of stiches went nearly all the way around her arm, as if the lower part had been wholly separated and then reattached.

Though Mom looked good and assured me it didn't hurt at all, she seemed lethargic. She didn't want to go out for lunch, so I went to the local deli and bought us a tuna sub to share, and potato chips. We ate in front of the TV, and then, before we went to Barbara's for dinner, Mom took a long nap. Over the four days of my visit, she improved only slightly.

I knew how trauma, especially cut or torn flesh, releases stress hormones that bring on fatigue. I supposed this was happening to Mom, and I remembered how her spirits and energy had flagged when she had broken her wrist ten years earlier. Back then, she had bounced back in a couple of weeks. This time, it took more than a month. Even with several weeks of physical therapy, she never returned to the Mom she had been before the fall.

She started asking Barbara to pick up groceries for her—something Mom used to do on her own, using the shuttle provided at McCarthy Court. She rarely went on the McCarthy field trips she had previously enjoyed; now, she only went if Barbara went along.

Joined Mom on the "geezer bus" for a tour of the Marine Corps Air Station at Cherry Point—great air show, Barbara wrote to me in an email.

Mom stopped reading books.

"The television keeps me entertained all day," she said.

She told me she wasn't going to vote anymore.

"I don't pay attention to any of the candidates. It just doesn't matter to me."

"Sounds reasonable to me," I replied. "You're ninety-two years old. You've done your part."

I told myself what I told Mom—that how she felt and what she did and didn't want to do seemed normal for her age. Intellectually, I knew this was true. Emotionally, I felt like I was watching her drift out to sea while I stood helpless on the beach. But it wasn't the tide that plagued Mom; it was gravity.

Through August, September, and October of 2008, she fell about once a week—though "fall" may be too strong a word. She would simply lose her balance while walking to the bathroom or kitchen, and then drift, fairly gently, to the floor. Unhurt, but also unable to get up on her own, she would press her "panic button" and ask the voice from the speaker to call the main office. One of the McCarthy staff would come to her apartment on the third floor and help her up. Barbara received a call after each and every incident. She started to dread the ringing phone.

Mom, on the other hand, didn't seem very upset by these falls. In fact, she was proud of her ability to handle them on her own. She bragged about the time she fell in the living room and didn't have her panic button around her neck.

"I crawled over to the apartment door, reached up and turned the knob, then held the door open with my shoulder and sat there. I knew someone would walk by and help me up."

"Sounds like you managed pretty well," I said, "but please wear the damned button! What if you had been hurt?"

Perhaps the most disturbing change during the fall of 2008 was that Mom stopped showering regularly. Both Barbara and I asked her about it.

"I don't do anything that makes me sweat," she explained, "I wash 'the critical spots' every day."

Mom kept a pint-sized pitcher, decorated with a cluster of purple grapes and two green leaves, on the back of the toilet. She filled it with warm water and used it in place of a bidet.

"Maybe she's too unsteady to wash in the shower," I said to Barbara.

"She has a shower chair—and there are handles on the walls."

"It takes a lot of energy to wash and dry off. Could she be that weak?" I asked.

"I don't know what it is, but I think it's time to get some help."

"Did you tell her that?"

"No, I was hoping you would do it. But I did find a service I think we can use. Check it out online. It's called Seniors Choosing to Live at Home."

We agreed that I would talk to Mom, and Barbara would coordinate everything.

I went to the website for Seniors Choosing...and liked what I saw. They offered services on a membership model—so much to join, then a flat hourly fee for personal care services (anything that involved touching, like bathing, feeding, and dressing) by a certified nursing assistant (CNA, or health aide), along with a lesser fee for non-personal care, like shopping, companionship, light housekeeping, or other chores.

Mom's response was predictable.

"I don't need any help," she said.

"Just let Barbara set you up with this agency, and see how it goes," I said.

"I can take a shower by myself."

"Okay, but at least someone would be there in case you fall. Please try this so I can stop worrying," I pleaded.

It took a couple more conversations, but she finally agreed to talk to them. Barbara signed her up, and Valerie, the owner of Seniors Choosing to Live at Home, came to do the mandatory assessment.

Mom was social by nature, and she didn't mind at all being the center of attention. I'd seen how she had perked up when we'd talked to the geriatric care manager back in Florida, and I imagined she had been equally charming when she'd met with Valerie.

"Mom told Valerie she did not need any help, but that it might be nice to have someone to visit with now and then," Barbara told me. "I made it clear that we needed someone who could be there when she showered, and maybe even help with that."

Barbara was impressed with the way Valerie got all the necessary information in a conversational way, and made Mom feel good about how much she could do on her own. By the end of the meeting, Mom had agreed to scheduling a home health aide twice a week, beginning that same week.

I heard almost nothing about the first two CNAs who visited Mom. I suppose they showed up and helped Mom shower and dress. Did they make the bed? Did they fix her a sandwich for lunch? I don't remember anything about them, and neither does Barbara.

And then came Dena.

Dena was a hundred pounds of sunshine in a candy-colored smock. She had a thick Southern accent and plenty to say. She wanted to know all about Miz Pratt (Mom, that is). Dena asked Mom about her girls, what she liked to eat, how she came to live at McCarthy Court, and where she had lived before. Dena told Mom about her two children, and about her own mother.

Mom got back into going to the recreation room for coffee and donuts.

"Because Dena likes to go," she told me.

Twice a week, Dena arrived at around 9:00 A.M., while Mom was enjoying her morning coffee. She made sure Mom had a shower, dressed, and got out and walked a little bit. Before she left, Dena made sure Mom had something ready to eat for lunch. And the whole time, according to Mom, they carried on a delightful conversation.

If Mom told Dena she didn't feel like a shower, Dena would insist.

"Miz Pratt, please don't get me in trouble with Barbara. She'll be mad at me if you don't have your shower," Dena told her.

She called Barbara with a report on every visit with Mom. Sometimes, when I called Mom's apartment, Dena would answer. And when we were on the phone, Dena did most of the talking.

We all loved her.

Meanwhile, Barbara became militant about trying to improve Mom's strength and balance. She talked to Dr. S., who ordered more physical therapy. Either Barbara or Dena would drive Mom to the clinic once a week, and Dena would help her do her exercises at home. Holding the kitchen counter, Mom would rise to her toes and then lower back down. Sitting in her chair, she would straighten one knee to lift her lower leg, then do the same on the other side. Barbara told Dena to make Mom walk for fifteen minutes—up and down the hall, or if the weather was nice, around the parking lot. Mom didn't like it.

"I told you, I'm allergic to exercise," she answered, when I asked why she had cancelled two physical therapy appointments.

"It's probably too little, too late," Barbara said, "after a lifetime of being a couch potato."

"But she used to be active," I replied. "Remember how she went on all the Girl Scout sleepovers, and set up tents and hiked with us?"

"Sure, like a hundred years ago!" Barbara sounded fed up.

Dena made Mom feel better and eased the burden on Barbara, but no one—not Dena, not even the physical therapist—could keep Mom from falling. I learned the hard way during my late October visit. I had gone up to the apartment to get Mom while Barbara and Phil waited in the car. We were headed out to dinner to celebrate Barbara's birthday.

Mom held the handrail as we walked down the hall. She took my arm, and we crossed to the elevator, where I pushed the "down" button. Suddenly, she sank to the floor, pulling on my arm as she went down. I couldn't hold her up, but I did slow her fall. I felt my face flush and then go pale.

"Are you alright?" I asked.

"Yes, fine."

"Are you sure? Do you feel weak or dizzy?"

"No, I'm fine. Just help me up."

I was shaking.

Over dinner, I told the story, trying to make light of it.

"Mom, you really should get a walker," Barbara said.

"I don't need a walker. I can walk just fine. I just lose my balance sometimes."

"And when you do, you could hang on to the walker, if you had one." I said. Mom accused us of spoiling the meal with all this negative talk.

Shortly after my October visit, Barbara sent an email update.

Took Mom out for lunch today. Before leaving the apartment, we went over the physical therapy bills because she was all confused about what to pay. When we got back from the restaurant, she started crying, saying how old and confused she feels. I decided I need to take over her bills, but I'm not going to tell her, I'm just going to go through the mail when I am there and take care of things.

I called to offer moral support.

"I feel so bad that there isn't more I can do. Do you want me to take over the bills?" I asked her.

"No, it would be too complicated to get them to you. I can handle it for now."

"Okay. Sorry it was such a tough day."

"Yeah. All of this bothers me, but not as much as it bothers her."

In November, four months after the fall in the recreation room, Mom fell again. She had gone into the kitchen to get a sandwich Dena had left for her. Somehow, both Mom and the sandwich ended up on the floor. With only three feet between the counters, there was no way she could avoid hitting something. She pushed her button and told the voice on the speaker she was hurt.

"I need someone from the office," Mom said.

The McCarthy Court staffer who came to help decided to call an ambulance, and then called Barbara.

Both Barbara and Phil met Mom at the emergency room.

"I'm not sure why we're at the hospital," Barbara said to me on the phone. "She only has a little scratch on her arm and a bruise on her wrist. I'm guessing the McCarthy staff just didn't want to take a chance. We're going to take her to our house for dinner."

Barbara continued our discussion the next day.

"How is she?" I was sitting at my desk in Miami.

"She's fine. She just takes these little falls in stride. When we got here last night, I put on a DVD of old *Jack Benny* shows. Mom watched from the leather lounge chair, and laughed and laughed."

"This is crazy," I said. "Why is she falling so much? I'm afraid she'll get hurt badly."

"I think it's time to look into moving her to Homeplace. Then, if she falls, someone will be there to help her right away. They have staff on duty all night."

Homeplace was the assisted-living facility affiliated with McCarthy Court, located just across the parking lot from Mom's building. At Homeplace, Mom would get three meals a day instead of one, and, for an additional fee, staff would help her shower and dress. She would have a lot more supervision—which appealed to me and Barbara, but I was pretty sure Mom wouldn't like the idea.

"Have you mentioned it to Mom?" I asked.

"She's adamant she doesn't want to move. I think the other McCarthy residents, especially Sophie, talk about moving to Homeplace as the kiss of death. Mom says she would never see her friends if she moved over there."

"It's across the parking lot, not across the state," I said.

"I know, but I guess it's like there's a Berlin wall between them."

"Well, why don't you find out what's available, or if there's a waiting list. I want to know what's possible before we bring it up with Mom."

After Barbara met with Kathy, the director at Homeplace, she became more convinced that Mom should move, because there was a rare two-room suite coming available in a couple of months. Mom would have a sitting room and a bedroom. Most Homeplace residents had just one room, in which they lived alone or with a roommate.

"You really think it's time?" I already knew the answer, but I hoped it wasn't so.

"I do. Anyway, better too soon than too late, right?"

I trusted Barbara's judgment. She saw Mom almost every day. I saw her only four times a year. And all the day-to-day care fell on Barbara, whether she was doing it or just managing it with the folks from Seniors Choosing to Live at Home.

"How hard can I push her?" Barbara asked.

"As hard as you want to," I said, "I'll support you a hundred percent."

I hung up the phone and wandered out to the Florida room. I found one of the cats lying in a wicker chair and sat down, pushing her to the side with my thigh. I reached down to scratch her ears and stared out at the bay. Mom had declined since July, but in many ways, she still seemed so capable. I didn't like that she spent so much time alone, but knew how much she valued her independence. Maybe it was too soon for assisted living—or maybe it wasn't. How could we know for sure?

Convincing Mom to move to Homeplace took me back two years to the battle for McCarthy Court. Barbara and I used well-honed weapons of reason and logic. We told Mom this was likely her only chance to get a two-room suite at Homeplace. We touted the comfort of three meals a day and additional help for whatever she might need, both now and in the future. Mom parried with her arsenal of arguments—that she was comfortable in her apartment, and had friends. Then she tossed a grenade.

"I just moved, and now you want me to move again?"

I cowered, and let Barbara lead the charge.

Barbara said, "It never hurts to look."

She and Mom toured the rooms in Homeplace, and had lunch there with Kathy. That afternoon, the three of us talked by phone.

"You're right. Homeplace is nice, but I have so much more room at McCarthy." Mom was digging in.

And you spend all your time in the living room or the bedroom, I thought.

"I'll move there one day, but not yet," she said.

The deadline to make a decision was a week away. Kathy had agreed to hold the suite for Mom, but we had to make the deposit by December 15th for a January 15th move-in date. Barbara threw her own grenade.

"Mom, it will be so much easier on all of us if you move now. Melanie and I worry about you all the time."

Mom agreed to consider moving. I circled back to push from another direction.

"If you know you're going to Homeplace at some point, why not do it now, when you can have a suite instead just one room? You know that Barbara and I will handle all the moving and make it as easy as possible."

"What about my friends? What about Dena?"

"Your friends will be right across the parking lot, less than a block away. And Dena can still come by to visit a couple days a week," I said, not knowing whether this was possible or not.

Barbara filled out all the forms, and after we gave each other a pep talk by phone, she went to visit Mom, who surprised us both by signing the papers. Barbara wrote the check and dropped everything off at Homeplace.

I expected to feel relieved—even happy. Instead, I felt sad and nervous. I was sure this would be Mom's last move. I took refuge in my lists—what should we move to make Mom feel at home? I wanted to help her adapt to Homeplace as quickly as she had to her McCarthy Court apartment.

A week later, Barbara called me, crying.

"She backed out."

"What happened?" I asked.

"I brought her some groceries and mentioned the move. She yelled at me; said she'd never agreed to go to Homeplace. She said I tricked her."

"Barb, I'm so sorry. You know this isn't your fault."

"I know, but she was so mean."

"She's scared. And maybe a little addled. Her short-term memory has been getting worse. Is it possible she really doesn't remember?"

"I don't know, but what do we do now?" Barbara sounded tired.

"What did you tell her?"

"I said I did not trick her, but I would see what I could do. Then I left, furious."

We decided we didn't have it in us to force her, so we'd give it a day or two and see how she felt. Barbara called Kathy at Homeplace and Diane at McCarthy Court to let them know things were up in the air, and to find out how much leeway we had. They both understood, saying these things happened fairly often. They gave us a few days to sort it out. It was my job to talk to Mom. Barbara needed some distance.

I waited two days—two long, short-tempered days. I thought Mom would call me. She didn't, so I called her. We exchanged *hellos* and *how're you doings*. She didn't mention Homeplace, and she didn't seem angry.

"Barbara says you've changed your mind about moving to Homeplace."

"Yes. I want to stay here." She didn't mention being tricked.

"I think Barbara is pretty upset." It seemed pointless to remind her that she'd agreed, and signed the papers. Had she forgotten what happened?

"I'm sorry. I don't want to move, and I don't think I should have to."

How much more can we take away from her? I thought. I wanted her to want what Barbara and I thought was best, but more than that, I wanted to let her decide on her own.

"Okay," I said.

Maybe it just wasn't time yet.

Chapter 13

Mom won the Homeplace battle, and stayed in her apartment at McCarthy Court. Barbara managed to get Mom's entire deposit back, and someone else moved into the suite at Homeplace. It would not be our last struggle to keep Mom safe while also trying to preserve her independence. Every time, a win for either side felt like a loss all around.

In early January of 2009, as I logged into the American Airlines website to buy my ticket to New Bern for Mom's 93rd birthday, Barbara called from the emergency room. Mom was bleeding from a cut on her head. She told the doctor she had slipped while getting out of bed and hit the bedside table.

"The doctor says Mom is entertaining. Personally, I am not amused." Barbara was understandably annoyed about another trip to the ER. "He also says she seems pretty healthy, especially given her age. They're going to do a CAT scan, and she probably needs a few stitches."

When we talked the next day, I asked about the results of the CAT scan.

"Nothing remarkable, just the expected change from a moist, plump brain to a shrunken raisin-brain."

I laughed. Mom's aged brain wasn't funny, but Barbara's delivery provided a much-needed spoonful of sugar for the bitter stew of Mom's decline.

I read the medical record for that visit to the ER after the fact. It described "an old lacunar infarct at the left basal ganglia"—evidence of a stroke. When had it happened? Could that have been the cause (or one cause) of Mom's recent falls? If the doctor had mentioned this to Barbara when they had been in the ER, she would have told me. I can only conclude that it hadn't come up.

By the time I arrived in New Bern the following week, Mom's stiches were out and her wound was nearly healed, but she had a bad cold. She was lethargic and cranky, barely interested in seeing me. I never got used to the way even minor illnesses affected her. When she got sick, or had an injury, she aged ten years. Then, after a prolonged recovery period, she'd "get younger" again, but never back to where she was before the episode.

Barbara and I talked to Mom about her falls, and insisted she get a walker.

"It's not my fault. I tell myself not to fall, but then I fall anyway."

"That's the point," I said, "you just need a little help with balance, and the walker will be perfect."

Her refusal made no sense to me. If the issue was pride or dignity, wasn't it more dignified to be standing than sprawled on the floor, waiting for a hand up? *Pride goeth before a fall*, I thought. Indeed!

"There's a medical supply store right around the corner," Barbara added, "and Medicare will pay for it." We knew we couldn't make her use it, but we were determined to put a walker within her reach. "Come on," Barbara said, "let's go pick one out, and then we can stop at the bagel shop for lunch."

"I don't feel like going out," Mom grumbled as she turned on the TV.

"Okay," I said, "We'll go get the walker and bring bagels back here." I stood up from the couch and dug my heels into the carpet.

"Bring me some coffee," she snapped. "They have good coffee there."

Buying the walker was easy once we saw how the different models worked. Barbara and I agreed that Mom wouldn't be able to manage the ones with brakes, and opted for the classic: aluminum frame, wheels on the front legs, rubber tips on the back legs. No seat, bells, or whistles. The clerk showed us how to adjust the height.

"Medicare will pay for at least part of it, right?" I wasn't sure about Medicare policies for medical equipment.

"It will, if the walker is ordered by the doctor," the clerk replied.

We didn't have an order from Dr. S., but Barbara said she could get one on Monday.

"I'll make a copy of your credit card and get all the Medicare insurance information. If you bring or fax the doctor's order on Monday, we'll bill Medicare directly. Otherwise, we'll charge the credit card," the clerk explained.

I thanked her for making it so easy.

"We do it all the time," she said.

Back at the apartment, we showed Mom how to use the walker, and made her take it down the hall to the bathroom and back.

"I do feel a little more stable." She *walkered* around the living room.

"Is this mine?" she asked.

"Yes," I answered, feeling confused about why she was confused. "We just got it for you. It's yours."

"Did I pay for it?"

"No. Medicare will pay for it." I left out the details. "Let's put your name on it." The other walkers in the McCarthy Court dining room were decorated with ID tags and colorful bows or scarves. Without these personal touches, they all looked alike. *If I ever need one*, I thought, *I'm painting on some flames or a lightning bolt.*

"Here, use this." Barbara handed me one of Mom's return address labels. Mom used to put them on the bottoms of trays and dishes she brought to potluck parties back at the New Port Richey condo.

I stuck the label on one of the bars of the walker, then guided Mom to the table for lunch. Barbara handed her the paper cup of coffee from the bagel shop.

"Oh, you didn't have to get this," Mom said, "I could have made coffee here."

She had already forgotten her snippy demand for coffee. It was one of those moments when I felt dragged down by her decline.

"It's a treat, Mom. I know you like their coffee." Barbara and I exchanged pained looks.

The walker sat in the corner, near the TV, not near Mom's chair. Over the next month, February of 2009, Barbara met Mom in the emergency room twice in one week. Both times, she told the doctor she had lost her balance and fallen, "as I often do." Both times, the medical notes described her thin skin, almost too thin for stitches. Both times, the notes mentioned how personable she was.

"I keep asking the doctors why she falls so much, but we see a different one every time we go to the ER," Barbara told me, "so it's hard for them to get the whole picture."

One ER doctor wrote that he had considered syncope—temporary loss of consciousness due to a drop in blood pressure—or a possible heart arrhythmia, or stroke; but then, without any testing, concluded it was a simple trip and fall.

"What does Dr. S. say?"

"He tells her to use the walker, and he orders more physical therapy."

"Tell the physical therapist to make her use the walker," I said, remembering Kate's advice about getting professionals to be the bad guys.

"I'm also going to get Seniors Choosing to send a health aide every morning. Dena will come most days, and someone else will come on Dena's days off. I don't want her dressing herself," said Barbara.

"Does she need help at night, too?"

"Probably, but I don't dare make too many changes all at once. She seems pretty depressed lately, and never goes out unless I take her."

"Or unless she goes to the ER."

"Yeah, funny, that's the only place she seems to perk up. I think she likes the attention."

That night, when Klein got home from work, he joined me in the kitchen, poured two glasses of wine, and turned on the news. I listened to the stories about a tornado in Oklahoma and a plane crash near Buffalo.

"Why do we watch this stuff?" I asked. "There's nothing we can do about it. It's so depressing."

"Honey, it's just the news. Do you want me to change it?"

"No, I know you like it." When he left to put on his comfy clothes, I switched to a Seinfeld rerun and concentrated on cooking.

I visited Mom and Barbara again the first week of April. Mom had managed to stay out of the hospital for nearly two months, and I could see why. She now used her walker every time she got up.

"It's my Cadillac!" she told me, "Look how fast I can walk."

Barbara confirmed that Mom's mood had improved over the last few weeks. Did the walker made her feel more mobile, more confident, less confined? Was it seeing Dena, who doted on her, five days a week? I didn't ask. I didn't care about why. I just enjoyed her happiness.

Barbara suggested another reason for the improvement in Mom's mood.

"She's getting less connected to everyday events—kind of in her own little world. Sometimes she calls to ask me what day it is."

"So, how would that make her happy?"

"I think she's getting to a point where she cares less about everything, including her confusion."

One thing she really cared less about was food. When we were growing up, Mom had prided herself on her cooking. Her everyday specials had included meat loaf, pork chops with tomato sauce, pot roast, and a delicious chicken *chow mein* she made with mostly canned vegetables. For dinner parties, she went all out with *boeuf bourguignon* or *Khoresh Bademjan*, an Iranian lamb stew. Barbara and I had both learned to love good food, and I still wanted to cook for Mom.

Hanging out at her apartment, I offered to make lunch.

"I want one piece of bologna on one slice of bread cut in half to make a sandwich," she said.

"No mustard? No mayonnaise?"

"No, just plain."

"I could fry the bologna, or add some cheese and make a toasted sandwich."

"No, I want it plain."

I made the plain sandwich—lunch for a four-year-old. Thinking about it, even now, makes me cry. But then she surprised me by asking to go out to dinner at a local restaurant.

"The crab cakes are wonderful," she told me.

After so many enjoyable meals with Mom at her dinner table and in restaurants, eating out with her had become painful. That night, Barbara and I struggled to pull Mom into some light banter, and worried about her clumsy use of silverware. When the meals arrived, our limited conversation stopped as Mom concentrated on her food. She leaned in to capture each bite, often losing half before the fork reached her mouth. Barbara and I kept chatting, and pretended not to notice the mess. After the meal, we gave the waitress an apologetic look and an extra-large tip.

That spring, as Mom's mood improved, mine tanked. Barbara's phone and email updates documented our mother's slow but continuous physical and mental decline.

"I called her at 3:30 to remind her about coming to dinner at my house," Barbara recounted. "When I got there at 5:00 to pick her up, she was sitting at her usual table in the McCarthy dining room."

"Was it on her calendar?" I asked. "She always checks the calendar."

"Mel, she calls me at least twice a week to ask what day it is. Yesterday, she also wanted to know what time it was."

In an email, Barbara wrote:

Dena gets there at 9 A.M., and more and more often, she finds Mom still asleep. I've increased her to three hours every morning, because now, in addition to getting Mom up and dressed, she also makes the coffee and toast. Plus, I still like for her to take Mom for a walk. I didn't even discuss it with Mom, and I don't think she noticed. Anyway, she loves having Dena around, and is even used to Oohna, who fills in on Dena's days off.

I hated being so far away. I wanted to do something to help. I wanted to be with Mom; I wanted to relieve Barbara. I worried, and had trouble concentrating. I jumped whenever the phone rang.

My household chores seemed endless, and I berated myself for not keeping up. Running out of butter, or milk, or coffee brought me to tears. And heaven help anyone who disappointed me. Klein took over all the interactions with customer service agents after I screamed at the cable provider when our Internet service was interrupted.

I would wake up early, try to focus on deep breathing, then give up and head into my home office. I'd bury myself in work until suddenly, mid-afternoon, I'd find myself with my feet up on the desk, staring blankly at Biscayne Bay. I pushed myself to exercise—an hour on the elliptical trainer while watching a funny or heartwarming movie.

One day, I figured out that Mom's bank offered online bill-pay. I called Barbara and told her I would take over the bills.

"Are you sure?" Barbara asked.

"Yes. Let me do this. Send me last month's bills so I can get it set up. Then when any new ones come, just tell me how much to pay and I'll do it all online."

"Okay, if you're sure."

"I am, unless it turns out to be harder on you. But let's try it."

The new system worked perfectly. Any payments with standard monthly amounts—McCarthy Court rent, Medicare and supplemental health insurance premiums—went out automatically, and Barbara would email me about the other bills, like electricity and phone. I finally felt a little more useful.

It was a warm night in early July when Barbara got a call from Shannon, one of the McCarthy staff. Mom had fallen in her closet while changing into her nightgown, then crawled around the bed, pulled the phone from the nightstand onto the floor, and called the front desk. The next day, Barbara told me the story.

"I drove over right away and helped her up."

"Shannon left her on the floor?"

"She stayed with Mom, but was afraid to lift her, afraid she might hurt her."

"How's Mom?"

"As usual, she's fine. Last night, she was shaky, and said she felt like a fool. I helped her get ready for bed, and told her I thought she was very resourceful to get to the phone the way she did. She was sleeping when I left."

I sighed, and slumped in my chair.

"Where was her panic button?" I asked.

"She hangs it on the bedroom door on her way in to get undressed."

"Ugh. What are we going to do?" I whined.

"I can't help wishing she was at Homeplace."

"We've got to get Dena or someone to come in at night."

"Don't even bring it up. I did, and she refused."

"Maybe it's not her choice anymore." I carried the phone to the Florida room and picked a few dead flowers off one of the potted plants.

"Look, this is the first fall in a while," Barbara said. "Let's see how it goes. If it gets bad again, we'll have a better chance of forcing the nighttime help."

For once, I thought it best that I wasn't in New Bern. I was furious with Mom. She was making it very hard for me to make her life easier.

A month later, Mom fell again while getting ready for bed.

"Let's just go ahead and book help for the evenings." Each fall chipped away my equanimity. How did Barbara stay on an even keel?

"I already sent the email to Valerie at Seniors Choosing. I'm going to tell Mom it's only for when I'm on vacation so she won't fight me."

Barbara and Phil were headed out on a two-week driving vacation through New England and Nova Scotia. I would be on call the full two weeks, and would go to New Bern and stay at Barbara's for eight days. Mom would be "alone" for a couple of days at the beginning, and a few more at the end of the vacation. It seemed like the perfect time to introduce nighttime care. In fact, it would be too late.

Chapter 14

I WAS IN PHOENIX PACKING UP to head back to Miami at the end of a business trip when my cell phone rang, and I saw Barbara's name on the screen. *Uh oh,* I thought. We were scheduled to talk the next day about my trip to New Bern to take over as local family caregiver while she went on vacation. This unplanned call could only mean bad news.

"We're at the hospital." Barbara's voice broke. "Mom had a bad fall last night, a really bad fall. Dena found her on the floor this morning, and the bed was still made from the day before."

"What happened?" This was my worst nightmare—Mom stranded on the floor for hours without help.

"I don't know. She's really confused. Dena found her naked. Her nightgown was in a heap beside her, and had pee and poop on it. When I got there, Dena was washing her up. We put on her clothes, and I brought her here to the ER."

"Jesus! Is she hurt? Did she have a stroke?"

"Look, I don't know. She's shaky. She couldn't walk by herself, even with her walker. She has some bruises on her left arm, shoulder and hip, and her left eye is swollen shut. That's all I can see. They're doing some tests."

I decided to cancel my morning meeting, change my ticket, and go straight to New Bern.

"Barb, I think I should come right away."

"No, we won't know anything more for a few hours. You can call me this afternoon when you get back to Miami."

"I don't know. It sounds really serious, and you seem pretty upset."

"I was afraid something would happen to ruin my trip," she sobbed. "I'm furious at her, and at myself. Why didn't I just insist on getting someone to come in at bedtime?"

"Look," I said, "This is not your fault. We'll figure it out. You will have your vacation."

I felt sick. As soon as I hung up, I got a cold washcloth from the bathroom and put it on the back of my neck. Despite what I told Barbara, I was sure this was our fault.

I broke the rules, and kept my cell phone on for the entire flight to Miami. A few minutes before we landed, I got an email from Barbara with more details.

What I found most frightening was Mom's confusion. She told Barbara she had been sleeping on the floor on purpose, because she was babysitting a pet bird for the people next door and didn't want to sleep in their bed. It must have been a weird dream, but she relayed it as if it were fact. She didn't remember falling.

I got off the plane, grabbed a seat in the gate area, and dialed Barbara's number. She was still at the hospital. Mom had been admitted for observation and monitoring.

"I had the night help set up for two days from now," Barbara moaned. "If only I had done it sooner."

"Stop beating yourself up," I said, as I mentally flayed myself. "We agreed not to force her. You're doing a great job, and you *are* going on vacation. If you and Phil can leave a day later, I'll come a day earlier, and she'll be safe in the hospital for the few hours neither of us is close by."

"But I'll be in Canada, and it will be hard to reach me." I could hear her anguish. She and Phil desperately needed this vacation, but Barbara didn't want to desert Mom.

"It's okay," I said, trying to convince myself by reassuring her, "I can handle it. You're there all the time. This is your break. I'll take charge."

Barbara emailed me three pages of notes. On the first page, she detailed the location of the keys to her house, Mom's purse, and food for Buster, the neighborhood cat who visited daily. On page two, she provided instructions for when and how to put out the trash, how to use the television, and how to check for messages on the phone. Page three was a list of phone numbers for neighbors, doctors, and Mom's physical therapist, along with addresses for the CVS where Mom got prescriptions and the Urgent Care Center.

I'll leave a folder on the kitchen counter with my gym card, super-market discount card, legal papers concerning Mom, and instructions for the espresso maker, she wrote.

She and Phil left Sunday morning, and I arrived in New Bern on Sunday afternoon at around 3 P.M. I drove straight from the Raleigh-Durham airport to the hospital.

I walked down deserted hallways, thinking this must be the quietest hospital on the planet. As I turned the corner toward the elevators, I was relieved to see a pink-jacketed volunteer sitting behind an information desk.

I asked for Eleanor Pratt's room number. The nice volunteer told me there was no one with that name in the facility. I squinted at her, and my brain searched for an explanation. *Is that possible? Could I be in the wrong hospital? If she's not here, how will I find her? Okay, breathe, think. I can't call Barbara. Wait—Mom's legal name is Mary Eleanor Pratt.*

"Try Mary Pratt," I said. Only complete strangers, like the hospital doctors and nurses, ever called her Mary.

"Yes," said the receptionist, "but are you sure it's the right person?"

"I'm sure," I snapped. "She's my mother. Can I go up?"

What will I do if I have to prove it? I thought. *My driver's license has my name as Melanie Pratt Merriman; will that work?* Then I remembered the healthcare proxy forms in my purse. I carried them all the time now.

Before I reached for the documents, the volunteer said, "Room 312."

I flushed, ashamed that I'd been short with her.

Mom was propped up in bed, dozing, her white hair flat and almost invisible on the pillowcase. The room was semi-darkened, lit only by the TV and slivers of late-afternoon sun coming through yellowed Venetian blinds. I touched her arm and kissed her cheek. She opened her eyes and smiled.

"Mel?" I was so relieved that she knew me. My eyes grew hot.

"How are you doing, Mom?" I smiled back at her.

"Alright, I guess. Where's Barbara?"

"She left on vacation." I knew Barbara had told her the night before. "I'll be here until she gets back."

"I'm so glad." Her voice was uncharacteristically soft.

I pulled the Naugahyde visitor's chair closer to the bed, and talked about my recent business trip until Mom dozed off. She seemed listless and looked banged up, but I was thinking about getting her to her apartment with some home health care. I could cook for her, and help her get her strength back. I went to the nurse's station to ask how long Mom would be in the hospital, and why she needed to be here.

The only useful thing Mom's nurse told me was that the doctor would be around to visit sometime the next day; she didn't know when. I assured her I would be there.

People in scrubs came in and out of the room. One helped Mom to use a bedpan; another checked her blood pressure, pulse, and temperature—all normal. Someone else brought her dinner around 5:00. Mom could hold the fork, but her hand shook. She let me feed her, which I found both alarming and soothing. At last, I was here when she needed me.

I couldn't get a clear reading on the situation. Based on the bedpan, it seemed that Mom couldn't—or shouldn't—get out of bed. Certainly, she seemed weak. But the initial tests hadn't shown evidence of a stroke or a heart attack. I hated waiting for answers.

At 7:30, *Jeopardy* came on the television. I stayed for about half the show, then told Mom I was getting tired.

"Is there anything you want? Anything else I can do for you tonight?" I asked her.

"No, no. You must be exhausted. Will you stay at Barb's?" I was grateful she seemed to be remembering what was going on.

"Yes," I said, kissing her. "I'll be back tomorrow, early."

I stopped at Harris Teeter for a bottle of wine and picked up some veggie lasagna from their prepared foods section. I had planned to buy groceries for the week, but was too tired to think about it. I pulled into Barbara's driveway and saw Buster, the big orange tomcat, waiting in the carport. I couldn't wait to sink my face into his fur.

I poured a glass of wine, heated my lasagna in the microwave, and tucked in on the couch with Buster and a movie. After another glass of wine, I fell asleep. At some point, I woke up, pulled up the afghan, set my phone alarm, and went back to sleep, fully clothed.

The next day, Monday, I was at the hospital at 7:45 A.M., cappuccino in hand, ready to be a good companion to Mom. I helped her eat some canned pears and sip some coffee.

"How is it?" I asked, pointing to the coffee.

"Terrible," she replied, "and cold."

I offered her some of my cappuccino and handed her a piece of toast.

Looking through all the papers on the bedside table, I found a menu.

"Hey, Mom," I said, "It says you can order anything you want for your meals. What would you like for lunch?"

"Can I have a hamburger?"

I called to place the order, and was told patients on the cardiac floor were not allowed to have red meat. *Cardiac floor?* I thought. *Is there something wrong with her heart?* Mom agreed to a turkey sandwich. Dietary restrictions for a ninety-three-year-old seemed ridiculous to me. I added a note about it to my growing list of questions for the doctor.

Mom and I watched one of the morning shows for a while. Then she wanted to use the bathroom. I rang for the nurse, who said she'd send someone to help with the bedpan.

"Why isn't she allowed to get up?" I asked. "I would think she needs to keep moving."

"The orders say she is confined to bed." Something else to ask the doctor about.

I pulled out my computer to finish analyzing some health-care-quality data I had collected for a client, and smiled at the irony.

"Mom, I'm going to do some work while we wait for the doctor. Okay?"

"Sure, sure. I'm just happy you're here," she said, still staring at the TV.

At around 10:00 A.M., I went out to the nurses' station to ask when the doctor was expected. No one knew.

Lunch arrived, and it was easier for Mom to eat a sandwich without help than to manage a fork. She insisted I eat half the sandwich and half the apple. It was just as well. I didn't dare leave to get some food until I talked to the doctor.

At 4:00 P.M., Mom's primary care physician, Dr. S., arrived. Mom greeted him warmly, as if he were a welcome visitor in her home. I almost expected her to offer him some coffee, or a snack. I had met him once before, but I reintroduced myself and launched into my questions.

"Why is she on the cardiac floor?" I asked.

"We're monitoring her heart to see if she is having episodes of missed heartbeats that could affect blood flow to the brain. It's possible her falls are being caused by mini-blackouts."

She had been falling for over a year, so I wondered why this hadn't been done before, but I didn't ask. I didn't want to seem aggressive or accusing.

"If that's the case, what can be done?"

"The cardiologist will come by later," he said. "He'll probably want to put in a pacemaker."

"A pacemaker?" *Had I heard him correctly?* He seemed so calm, but I felt like the whole room was spinning. I had been prepared to drive this conversation with my questions about how long she needed to be hospitalized, possible changes to her medications, and follow-up care. Now I felt like I'd been tossed into the back seat with no view out the windshield. I didn't even know where to start the discussion.

"Will that really help?" I asked.

"Let's see what the cardiologist says, then we can talk some more."

"You said he's coming today?" I asked, surprised and worried that there was not much more of the day ahead of us.

"Yes," Dr. S. replied. He turned and took Mom's hand. "I'll be back tomorrow."

"Thank you," I said, wondering what I was grateful for.

Then, right after he left, I remembered about the dietary restrictions. I hurried after him.

"Surely, at this point in her life, she can eat whatever she wants—right?" I asked.

He agreed, and said he would change the orders.

Dr. B., the cardiologist, showed up at 6:30, after Mom's dinner. She was drowsy, but gave him a big smile. His Southern gentleman's drawl sounded phony. He sat on Mom's bed and took her hand. It struck me as too familiar, too fast. I wanted to trust him, but I needed information, not empty gestures.

He showed us the tracing from the heart monitor. It was easy for me to see that Mom's heart was skipping a beat or two, much too often. Dr. B. did not suggest this might be normal for a ninety-three-year-old heart.

"I think we should insert a pacemaker," he said. "I've ordered an echocardiogram for tomorrow, and I'd like to do the surgery on Wednesday."

Mom said, "No, I don't want it."

They were both way ahead of me. *No decisions without facts.* I asked why he thought she needed a pacemaker. He explained that it might help prevent another fall.

"Because it would improve blood flow to her brain?" I ask.

"Yes," he said. "The skipped beats can cause dizziness, or even fainting."

"But she's not fainting."

"Still, I think this could help."

Mom was quiet. Neither Dr. B. nor I asked her why she didn't want the pacemaker.

I told Dr. B. we would need some time to decide, and he promised to come back the next day and answer any questions we had.

"Don't worry," he said, patting Mom's hand, "I do these procedures often, and on people even older than you."

And then he was gone. I made a note to ask him if those procedures he mentioned had been successful.

I helped Mom brush her teeth, and stayed with her until she was asleep. As soon as I was in the car, I called Barbara's cell phone. I had no idea whether or when she might get the message. Then I called Klein to tell him about the pacemaker.

"I feel blindsided," I said. "I need to get on the Internet and try to learn more about pacemakers. Does this count as prolonging her death, which I know she doesn't want, or is it going to improve her life?"

"I don't know," he replied, "but it sounds like that's the right question."

Everything I found on the Internet suggested that pacemaker insertion was safe, even for the elderly. The procedure is done under "twilight sedation"—like they use for colonoscopies—not full-blown anesthesia, which I knew to be more dangerous. I read comments from people whose parent had received a pacemaker. Some had seen improvements in function; some hadn't. At least there were no horror stories.

Mom had always been clear about not wanting to artificially pro-long her life. For more than a year, she'd told us she was "ready to go," but didn't seem close to death. And if she was going to live a year or more, I wanted to do anything that would make that time the best it could be. Even minor surgery could be traumatic, and I had seen how a simple cold could hit Mom hard. Would the surgery shorten her life? I was pretty sure I could live with that if the shorter time was better time—better than it had been with all these falls. What if she died on the table? I would feel responsible. How could I not? But I just didn't think it would happen.

I wrote out a new list of questions. I needed to confirm that we were talking about a pacemaker that would simply regulate her heartbeat, not a defibrillator that would shock her back to life if her heart stopped. I wanted to be sure she could die naturally with the pacemaker in place. I wanted promises that if anything went wrong during the surgery, they would let her go; that her "do not resusci-tate" request would be honored. Most of all, I wanted assurances that with the pacemaker, she would feel better, have more energy, and fall less often.

I crawled into bed at midnight. I lay in bed doing yogic breath-ing, but my mind wouldn't quiet. After an hour or so, I got up and emailed two colleagues who were also friends—Ira, the palliative care physician with whom I'd co-authored the quality of life index, and True, a nurse and hospice expert—asking for advice. They were perhaps the wisest and most soulful healthcare professionals I knew.

At close to 2 A.M., I wrote up a plan for my conversation with Mom. I created talking points the way I would for a business presentation:

- Assure Mom that this is her decision, and that I will support her no matter what she wants;
- Acknowledge understanding that she does not want "heroics;"
- Lay out the positives—simple surgery, possible improvement in thinking, fewer falls or no falls;
- Lay out the negatives—surgery and recovery;
- Ask about her questions/concerns.

Unable to think of anything else I could do for the moment, I finally slept for a few hours.

Both Ira and True sent replies by 8 A.M. Both offered condolences and support. Ira assured me that Mom could die a natural death, even by heart attack, with the pacemaker in place. True said pacemakers are very common even in older people, and commiserated with the dilemma of the adult child trying to do what's right for the parent. Both said they were confident I would make the right decision. Was there a right decision? I saw two choices: the harder one, not to agree to the pacemaker; and the easier one, to let the doctors do what they wanted. Neither one felt right.

I greeted Mom around at 8:30 with some freshly-sliced bananas and strawberries I had fixed before I left Barbara's. While she finished eating, I sat on the bed and started the discussion. "Mom, we need to decide about the pacemaker. You said you don't want it, but what if it could help with your falls?"

"I don't know," she said and closed her eyes. "It's almost too hard to think about it."

"Are you scared?" I asked.

"No. I just don't understand it all."

What had I been thinking? She couldn't make this decision. And really, would I have trusted any decision she made? She was the one who didn't think she needed evening care. I had to accept that the choice really was in my hands—and my hands were shaking. I wished Barbara would call.

We sat in the room all day, Mom watching TV with eyes half-closed, and me trying to focus on analyzing survey comments. Maybe it looked like I was working, but all I was really doing was waiting for that cardiologist, Dr. B. I made sure the nurses knew that I needed to talk with him.

At around 10 A.M., I looked up from the computer just as Dena walked into the room.

"Hey, Miz Pratt. I had to come see you, 'cause I missed you too much," Dena sang, a smile covering her face. Mom lit up. Why hadn't I thought to call her? She must have been worried.

"Dena!" I jumped up and gave her a hug. "What a wonderful surprise."

The three of us visited for a while, and I filled Dena in on the plan for surgery the next day. She didn't have a cell phone, so I gave her my phone number and told her to call me anytime.

"Now, don't you worry," she said to Mom. "I know you're gonna do just fine. And I'm gonna pray for you."

"Can you stay for a few minutes while I go outside to make a call?" I asked Dena.

"Sure," she said, "You take your time."

When I got back, I asked her to visit again as soon as she could. I told her I would call Seniors Choosing to set it up—my subtle way of letting her know she would be paid. She was "family," but I was pretty sure she couldn't afford to give away too much of her time.

Right after Mom's lunch, the hospital discharge planner stopped by the room. She told me Mom was scheduled for a pacemaker implant the next morning. I told her it would not be decided until we saw the doctor.

"Well, we've arranged for her to be discharged to the rehab center on Thursday," she said.

Mom hadn't even had the surgery yet, and the hospital was already planning for her discharge. This was a part of healthcare I understood from my hospice work. Mom's "case" would be given a code (from the *International Statistical Classification of Diseases and Related Health Problems*, or ICD-9) that would determine the amount Medicare would pay the hospital. The payment would be based upon a predetermined number of days, plus specific amounts for "medically necessary" procedures. The discharge planner was responsible for making sure Mom would leave the hospital within the timeframe covered by Medicare, and not stay a moment longer.

None of this bothered me. In fact, I was relieved that Mom was in line to go for rehabilitation. After five days in bed, and with what I had seen of her debility, she would need it, whether she received a pacemaker or not.

"Will she go for rehab even if she doesn't have the surgery? I mean, she can't walk, at this point. I believe Medicare will pay for a certain period of rehab, right?" I was feeling pretty good about my Medicare knowledge—thanks to my years in hospice.

"You would need an order from the doctor indicating that she needs skilled nursing care, but yes, I am pretty sure she would be eligible," the planner replied. We agreed to talk again the next day, when the decision about the pacemaker had been made.

Around 3 P.M., Barbara called, and I brought her up to date about what I knew, fuming about not having seen the doctor yet.

"I am leaning toward doing it. It just doesn't seem like she has much of a life right now. If the pacemaker can make it even a little bit better...." My thoughts trailed off.

"I'm worried about putting her through surgery," said Barbara.

"I worried about it, too, but it's fairly minor—and she won't be under general anesthesia."

I could tell Barbara was against the surgery, and I wanted to respect her position. I didn't want to act like the out-of-touch, out-of-town family member who swoops in and undermines the hard-working day-to-day caregiver. I wasn't out of touch, though, and I had thought this through. I told Barbara I didn't expect a miracle.

"I know what we get if we don't do it—she'll be the same," I said. "Even with more help, she'll continue to fall, and probably end up back here. At least with the pacemaker, there's some potential for improvement."

"Look, Mel, I'll support whatever decision you make. I agree that it probably can't hurt. I just don't have much hope it will make her better," Barbara said.

"Maybe it will slow her decline."

It would be some time yet before I understood that once decline has become irreversible, faster is better.

After I talked with Barbara, I left the room to get a snack. I was gone ten minutes. When I returned, a nurse I had not yet met told me that Dr. B. had visited, and confirmed that Mom was scheduled for pacemaker placement the following morning.

"No," I blurted out. "He assured us we would have a chance to ask questions. Is he coming back?" I fought back frustration and tears as she told me he had left the hospital for the evening.

"Please," I said. "Can you get him on the phone? I have to talk to him."

Thirty minutes later, Dr. B. walked into the room. I was grateful, relieved, and furious that he had been planning to go ahead without talking to me. I wanted to appear confident and commanding, but my voice shook with emotion as I asked my questions.

His answers were glib. "She'll be fine. I do this all the time. Don't worry."

I saw no sign that he had thought about Mom as a unique individual. She was just another place to put a pacemaker.

"What if we decide not to do it?" I asked.

"There's no reason not to," he replied.

He seemed to have no doubts, while I had nothing but.

I wanted to scream at him. *Help me decide what's best for her—this special person to whom I owe so much. She's ninety-three and confused, but she said she did not want it. Can't you see how hard this is?*

Instead, I sank onto the bed and took Mom's hand. My own weakness surprised and frightened me. I wasn't strong enough or brave enough to fight his complete certainty. And I wasn't ready to act as if her life were over.

"Mom, I think we should go ahead with the pacemaker. Is that okay?"

"Yes, honey. If you think it's a good idea, let's do it."

I knew her agreement was hollow. Still, I allowed myself a moment of reprieve.

Chapter 15

THE SURGERY WAS SCHEDULED FOR 10:00 A.M. The nurse came to Mom's room around 9:00, followed by an orderly pushing a gurney. I gathered up my purse and computer while they prepared Mom for transport, and then we all made our way to the surgical area. At the big double doors, the orderly pointed the way to the waiting area, and told me to check in with the volunteers.

"We'll take good care of her," he said.

I leaned over the bed and gave Mom the best hug I could.

"I love you, Mom. I'll see you when you're done." I believed she'd come through okay, but who could know?

"Don't worry, honey, I'll be fine." Mom was nothing if not a trouper. I remembered how she'd joked with the orderly who had wheeled her into the room where Daddy, Barbara, and I were waiting after her mastectomy.

"What kind of surgery did you have?" the orderly had asked her.

"They cut my boob off," she replied with a smile.

With the now-stringent healthcare privacy laws, you never heard that kind of friendly banter anymore.

The surgical waiting room in the New Bern hospital was ringed with hard plastic straight-backed chairs facing the center of the room. I blinked as my eyes adjusted to the harsh lighting. The volunteer sitting at a large metal desk in the center of the room asked for my name and Mom's name. I reminded myself to refer to Mom as Mary Pratt. The volunteer handed me an information sheet and pointed to the single-serve coffeemaker on an adjacent table.

"We'll pass on any updates we get from the surgical suite," she said. "If you have questions, just let me know."

"Can I use my cell phone?" I asked.

"No. We have a phone, but it's only for local calls," she replied.

Surprisingly, there was a Wi-Fi connection—the first and only one I'd encountered at the hospital. I decided to work through my email. For the last few days, I'd limited myself to high-level triage on incoming messages, letting the less urgent ones pile up. Now I had almost two hundred emails in my inbox. I looked at the clock: 9:30 A.M. If they started Mom's surgery on time, at 10 A.M., and if it took an hour, as I'd been told, then I wouldn't hear anything until 11:00 or so—about an hour and a half away. I told myself to wait two hours before starting to worry, and dove into the messages from the outside world.

I managed to focus for about ten minutes at a time. I checked the clock, and checked it again. Fifteen minutes short of my two-hour goal, I couldn't think about anything except the time. At 11:45, I asked the volunteer if she could get an update. A few minutes later, she told me Mom was in recovery, and the doctor would be out soon to talk to me.

"Is she all right?" I asked.

She rifled through the pages on her clipboard, and then scribbled a check mark on one of them. "They just said she's in recovery."

I told myself that was good news; if anything had happened, she would still be on the table, or on her way to ICU. I watched the clock for another fifteen minutes, and just as I was about to ask for another update, Dr. B. came through the door and scanned the waiting room. I waved him over.

"She did fine." He remained standing, so I had to tilt my head up to see his face.

"Why did it take so long?" I asked, my voice tight.

"We just got started a little late," he said, finally sitting in the empty chair beside me. I was relieved, and angry that no one had told me sooner.

Dr. B. explained that the pacemaker would be monitored remotely. He said something about a bedside base station and sending data to the pacemaker company. I nodded without really understanding.

"Call my office and make an appointment for two weeks from now, and the technician will give you the equipment and show you how to set it up," he said.

Again, I nodded. Did I need to know all this now? I'd look it up later. I made a quick note to call his office for the appointment.

"Do you have any questions?" Dr. B. asked.

"I know she's scheduled to go for rehab, and that Dr. S. will be managing her care. Do you do any kind of follow-up?" My irritation probably showed, so I tried to cover. "I mean, is this the last time we'll see you?"

"I'll stop by tomorrow to be sure everything's alright. I'm not worried. She did great." He smiled and looked at his watch.

I still felt like I was missing key information, but I had no idea what to ask. At this point, I just wanted to see Mom. Dr. B. stood up, signaling that the conversation was over.

"Thank you," I said. It was a reflex. I imagined Dr. B adding Mom to his list of "successful" cases.

After he left, I realized I didn't know what happened next, or where I was supposed to go. The volunteer told me I should go back to Mom's room and wait for her there. Before I left the Wi-Fi connection, I emailed Valerie at Seniors Choosing and Diane at McCarthy Court to let them know about the pacemaker and Mom's upcoming transfer to the nursing home for rehabilitation. I asked Valerie to schedule Dena for a visit to the hospital the next day, and told her we'd also like to have Dena come see Mom in rehab. Dena was Mom's happiness tonic, and frequent doses seemed like a good idea.

On my way back to Mom's room, I picked up a sandwich and some yogurt at the coffee shop. I didn't want to leave her until the evening.

I watched Mom even more closely than usual to see how the surgery had affected her. She said she felt fine, but then she asked me why she had a bandage on her chest.

"That's where they put in the pacemaker," I told her.

"Oh, is it all over, then?"

"Yes, all over." I hoped her confusion was a temporary side effect of the sedation.

She denied any pain, the same way she had done after every fall. I wondered if her pain nerves were wearing out along with the rest of her body, but also suspected they'd given her some good painkillers during or immediately after the procedure. She hadn't had anything to eat since the night before, so I asked if she was hungry.

"What time is it? Can I have breakfast?" she asked.

"It's almost 1:30. Maybe we could get you an omelet. Would you like that?"

"That sounds good, and some toast."

I checked with the nurse. She said it was all right to give Mom whatever she wanted to eat, so I called the kitchen and ordered a cheese omelet and whole-wheat toast. Mom napped until the food came. With my help, she ate almost half the eggs and a few spoonfuls of my yogurt.

For the rest of the afternoon, Mom and I settled into the usual hospital routine—various nurses or nursing assistants came in and out of the room to check her vital signs, help her use the bedside commode (she'd graduated from the bedpan), ask about her pain level (still zero), and give her medication. Mom watched TV, nodding off now and then. Not so different from her days at home, I thought, except that she was clearly much more debilitated. I worked in fits and starts, grateful for a straightforward data-sorting task that took enough attention to keep me feeling productive, but didn't require much brain power. When Mom was awake, we chatted about not much at all.

At around 3:30, the discharge planner stopped by. She confirmed that Mom would go to the nursing home affiliated with the hospital for rehabilitation. Dr. S. was on staff there.

"We'll take her over tomorrow, probably in a wheelchair, as soon as Dr. B. signs her release," she told me.

"Are you familiar with the place?" I asked.

"They have a great rehab program," she replied.

I asked the question that seemed to get the best information out of healthcare providers.

"Would you want your own mother to go there?"

"Yes, if my mother needed inpatient rehab, I would be fine with having her there."

That was good enough for me.

Mom's dinner arrived a little after 5:00. The only thing she wanted was the ice cream, and she ate the entire Dixie cup by herself.

"That was good," she said. "Can I have more?"

"Why not?" I answered, laughing. I knew they kept some at the nurse's station. After the stress of the last several days, I loved seeing her enjoy something, anything.

Before Mom had finished her second Dixie cup, Dr. S. stopped by to check on her. He told her she looked great, and Mom told him she felt fine. I had to give her credit; even if she wasn't sure what had happened, she was taking it all in stride.

"Well, now we need to build up your strength and get you walking again," he said.

"I can probably walk," she said. "I just don't have my walker."

"I'm not so sure, Mom," I said, trying to telegraph to Dr. S. that she didn't have a clue. I had seen how hard it was for the nursing aide to get her out of bed to use the bedside commode. Even if the pacemaker worked to prevent temporary blackouts, her wobbly legs would barely support her.

He seemed to understand perfectly.

"I want you to have some intensive physical therapy. So tomorrow, we'll transfer you to the nursing home across the street," he said.

I explained that we had talked with the discharge planner, and asked how long he thought Mom would be in rehab.

"At least a week," he said. "We'll have to see how it goes."

That meant I needed to start looking into care options for her at McCarthy Court. I decided to wait until Friday, after she was settled at the nursing home.

Dr. S. squeezed Mom's hand, and said the next time he saw her would be at the nursing home. He acted as if everything was going to be all right, but I was still on high alert. It occurred to me that he probably took care of lots of people like Mom. This was my first time, and she was my only mother.

Dr. B. came by early the next day, around 8:30 A.M. I was there, with my cappuccino and a cup of regular coffee for Mom. He and the nurse removed the dressing from Mom's surgical site.

"It's a little red," he said. "Does it hurt?"

"No," she answered.

"I'd like to keep you here another day, just to make sure everything is all right. Is that alright with you?"

"I'd rather go home," Mom answered, "but if you think I need to stay, I'll stay."

"So, everything pushes back a day?" I asked. I wanted to get Mom moving. I'd read that it could take a week of rehab for an older person to recover from a day in the hospital, and Mom had been in that bed for six days. And honestly, we both needed a change of scenery.

"Yes, I think that's best," he said. "I'll check in again tomorrow morning, but I don't expect any problems."

He told the nurse to put a clean dressing on the wound, continue the antibiotics, and contact the Discharge Planning Department about the change in orders. I resigned myself to another day in the hospital.

I wrote an email update for Barbara and Klein, and just as I finished, Dena arrived. I don't know who was happier to see her—Mom or me. She fussed over Mom, telling her how good she looked. Mom even muted the TV so she could chat.

"You'll be home in no time, Miz Pratt," Dena cooed.

I told her about the plans for a week or more in the rehab facility, and said I wanted her to visit Mom there.

"You know I will," she said. "I'll do anything I can to help."

I took the chance to leave Mom with Dena, and went outside to catch a cell phone signal and send the email to Barbara and Klein. Then I decided to go for a short walk. I was used to working out almost every day, and the lack of exercise had compounded my stress. Gray clouds covered the hot August sun, but even the humid air felt fresh after being cooped up in the hospital for days. Thank goodness Barbara had found Dena.

I saw the nursing home, and thought I should stop in for a quick check. What would I do if I didn't like it? What alternative was there? I decided to keep walking and hope for the best.

When I got back, Mom's lunch had arrived—the hamburger she'd wanted for days. I heard myself making much too big a fuss over a lukewarm, skinny little burger. Then again, Mom seemed to enjoy it.

At 2:00, I headed downstairs to the coffee shop to make a business call. The benefit and the burden of being self-employed was that I could—and did—work from anywhere. Having colleagues and clients who dealt with caregiving as part of their work, and often in their personal lives, as well, helped. Compassion was essential in our work, and most of us had an abundance to share.

On the way back to the room an hour later, I said hello to the discharge planner who was sitting at the nurse's station.

"Oh, good," she said. "I need to talk to you. There's no bed available at the nursing home where your mother was supposed to go."

"I thought it was all set." I dreaded the thought of another day in the hospital.

"It was all set for today, but now that she's not leaving until tomorrow, they've given it to someone else."

"So, what happens now?" I asked.

"Well, we have to find a bed somewhere else. There are two other nursing homes. Do you have a preference?"

"What? I don't know anything about them. I don't even live here." Was she really expecting me to make this decision? I wondered if it was too late to go and see the two options.

Somehow, the professional part of my brain kicked in. I had been working on quality measures for hospices, and I remembered that similar measures were already in place for nursing homes. Medicare had a website (www.medicare.gov/nursinghomecompare)* where I could look at the quality data for nursing homes anywhere in the U.S. I had never used it, but it was just what I needed.

"Wait," I said, "I need to get on the Internet. Then I can choose."

I knew I could access the Internet in the surgical waiting room, so I grabbed my computer and found my way back there. I was prepared to argue my way in, but no one stopped me. The website was easy to use—search for nursing homes by zip code, then click on the ones you wanted to compare. There were three in New Bern, and a few others within a twenty-mile radius. I decided to start by comparing the three in New Bern—the one Mom was now shut out of, and the other two. The website provided ratings based upon health inspections, staffing (hours of staff time per patient), and quality measures (like pain management, percentage of patients with bedsores, and appropriate use of medications). One home rated higher than the others on the things that mattered most to me—even higher than the facility where Mom had originally been scheduled to go. Maybe this apparent snafu would work to our advantage.

I headed back upstairs and told the discharge planner I thought Beechwood Nursing & Rehabilitation Center looked best to me. She confirmed the choice, telling me they had a new rehab wing that was quite nice. I hoped they would have a bed. Ten minutes later, she came to Mom's room and let me know it was all set. Mom would be transferred to Beechwood via wheelchair van the next day.

---

*Medicare also has websites to compare hospitals, physicians, home health services, dialysis facilities, and other healthcare service providers. Much of my work contributed to developing measures for a Medicare hospice comparison website.

Chapter 16

I KNEW A LOT ABOUT NURSING HOMES, or "nursing facilities" as they are more often called in healthcare circles, because hospice care is delivered to patients wherever they live—even if they live in a nursing home. I had spent time in nursing facilities in several states, dating back to my first days as a hospice employee, when I studied the delivery of hospice and palliative care to residents.

I knew that nursing facilities have two primary lines of business: short-stay rehabilitation for post-hospitalization patients who need to regain function after hip or knee replacements, heart attack or other serious illness—and, like Mom, pacemaker insertion—and long-term-care patients who will reside in the nursing facility for the rest of their lives. Medicare pays well for the rehab patients, though only for a limited number of days; nursing facilities want as many rehab patients as they can get. Medicare does not pay for long-term residential care (LTC), and neither does private insurance (except for some long-term-care policies). Most LTC patients have their room and board paid for by Medicaid because, almost always, these are people who do not have enough money to live somewhere else. People with money for assisted living or a board-and-care home (or any other option) will rarely, if ever, choose to live in a nursing facility.

I knew quite a bit about nursing homes, but I had no idea what it was like to stay in one. I was about to learn a lot more than I ever wanted to know.

Mom and I arrived at Beechwood on Friday afternoon. I drove over on my own ahead of the wheelchair van and filled out all the paperwork. The first thing I learned was that Mom's status as a short-stay rehab patient did not guarantee her a room in the bright, newly renovated, nicely furnished private rooms in the rehab wing. The intake coordinator explained that Mom would be in a double room in the long-term-care wing until a rehab bed opened. I asked if we could have a single room. I wanted Mom to have a little more privacy, and the freedom to get up early or turn her television up loud.

"If it costs more, we'll pay the extra," I said.

"The cost is the same," the coordinator told me, "but there are no single rooms right now. She'll probably be moving early next week, as soon as a rehab room opens up. I'll note that she prefers a single room."

I thanked her and signed eight to ten different documents. I wondered how this worked if there were no family members to read and sign everything.

I met Mom at the curb as the van driver lowered her in her wheelchair to the sidewalk. Then I followed behind as the coordinator wheeled her down a corridor that could only be described as "institutional"—drab gray/green walls, a gray linoleum floor, and dim fluorescent light. I sniffed—no urine or mold smells, just a vague odor of disinfectant and cafeteria food. The hallway was decorated with several residents in wheelchairs. I noticed two women who looked like sisters, both wearing sweaters in pastel colors that reminded me of sherbet. I smiled at them and they smiled back. I listened to the eerie quiet punctuated by an occasional staccato request from one aide to another, or the sing-song voice of a nurse encouraging someone to take pills the way a mother might coax her child to eat a few more bites of spinach.

At the end of the hallway, we turned into a room on the left. Late-afternoon sunlight from a single large window turned the light blue walls a pale, almost soothing, lavender. The room held two hospital-style beds with railings and electronic controls to adjust the height of both the head and the foot; two over-the-bed rolling tables; a small metal chest of drawers; and two closets. Mom's bed was by the window. Next to the other bed, a woman sat in a wheelchair. She listed to the right, with her elbow on the arm of the chair and her right hand on her forehead.

"This is Becky," said the coordinator, gesturing toward the woman in the chair. "And Becky, this is Mary," she continued. I let that one pass, making a mental note to post a note that Mom was called Eleanor.

"I'm Melanie," I said to Becky, "her daughter."

"I'm not feeling very well," said Becky.

"I'm sorry," I said. "We'll try to be quiet."

The coordinator pointed out the call button on the bed controller and showed us the bathroom. She explained that rehab patients were expected to come to the dining room for dinner, but Mom could have dinner in her room tonight if she preferred. I told her we would let them know.

I asked when Mom would have her rehab assessment, and that's when I learned that Friday was the worst possible day to arrive at a nursing facility. There were no rehab services on the weekends, so Mom would not have a care plan or even be assessed until Monday. That meant we were just biding time for two full days. And then came my next lesson—televisions are not provided in LTC rooms at Beechwood. There are cable outlets, but you have to provide your own set and fill out a form to order and pay for the service yourself. The intake coordinator explained the process—the maintenance crew would hook it up, but I couldn't put in the request until Monday—and maybe I should wait, because Mom was likely to move to a different room. Now we were looking at a weekend without rehab services or entertainment. If I wanted to make the best of this situation, I had my work cut out for me.

Mom needed to use the bathroom, so we pushed the call button. Fifteen minutes later, I decided I'd better try to help Mom myself. Thankfully, the nursing aide showed up just as we were trying to figure out how to transfer from the wheelchair to the toilet. I mentioned we had waited a long time.

I heard the aide tell a coworker, "They don't understand; this isn't like the hospital."

I hadn't meant to complain or be rude, but how was I to know what to expect? Had I missed the orientation session? Was Mom supposed to ring the bell fifteen to twenty minutes before she had to pee?

These nursing aides are overworked and underpaid, taking care of people who rarely show gratitude, I reminded myself. And I wanted them to like me. No, I wanted them to like Mom, and be nice to her. In the coming months, I would learn that many of them worked two jobs—two full shifts, most days—both here and at another facility.

I aimed to be the model family member. I would learn the names and faces of all the nurses and nursing aides. I would greet them, whether I needed anything or not. I would thank them for every service. I would ask them to explain the rules. Over time, I hoped, they would thaw.

Both Mom and Becky decided to have dinner in the room. Mom said she was tired. Becky said she probably wouldn't eat at all. She seemed miserable.

I went to the nursing station to make sure Mom's medications had arrived from the pharmacy, and that they had the discharge orders from the hospital. Communication in these transitions from one care setting to another can be dismal—critical information gets misplaced, mistakes are made, patients go for too many hours without needed medications. I wanted to be sure Mom would get her antianxiety medication, Xanax, this evening, and her antidepressant, Lexapro, in the morning. I was prepared to go to her apartment and get them, if necessary, even though I knew I'd have to sneak them in—no outside medications are allowed in hospitals or nursing homes.

Susanna, the nurse at the desk, told me to check with Louise, the nurse who was in the hallway distributing medications. I interrupted her as politely as I could, calling her by name, and she assured me that Mom would get all of her meds on time—but she hadn't actually checked the cart. I had Xanax with me, so the evening was covered. I decided to get some Lexapro from Mom's apartment and bring it over in the morning.

Just as the dinner trays arrived, Mom needed to use the bathroom again. I had paid attention to the earlier bathroom ballet, and I was ready to try it on my own:

Aim the wheelchair toward the wall with the grab bar. Once Mom has hold of the grab bar, push gently on her back so she can stand; slide the chair back; then help her lower her pants and ease down onto the toilet seat. Leave the room to give her some privacy, but stay close by. When she's finished, get her to grab the bar again, and help her to stand. Use the large, damp wipes from the box on the back of the toilet to clean her up. Pull up her pants, push the wheelchair close, and lock the wheels. Standing behind the chair, put your arms under her arms to brace her as she sits.

"Well, I never thought you'd be wiping my butt for me," said Mom.

"It's only fair," I replied. "You did it for me. I owe you."

I fought unease and sadness. *If I can be comfortable, or at least act comfortable, doing this*, I thought, *then Mom can be comfortable, too.*

We danced that dance over and over in the following months. It became routine, but it always felt unnatural.

By 6:15, dinner was over. Looking for a way to be helpful, I carried the trays into the hallway and placed them on the rolling rack for return to the kitchen. True to her word, Becky had eaten almost nothing. Mom had a better appetite, and happily, she had been able to feed herself with just a little help cutting up her slice of ham.

Mom wanted to get into bed. I felt like I needed to ask permission, so I rang the bell. Renee, one of the aides, came, and the two of us helped Mom change into the clean nightgown I'd brought to the hospital that morning. I was pleased to see that the scrapes on Mom's knees from her big fall were getting better.

"Does she usually wear a diaper at night?" Renee asked me.

"No, I do not," Mom answered.

I was close to tears. I was thinking about how long it might take for an aide to get to her if she had to get up in the middle of the night. *Which would be worse?* I thought. *For me to suggest she wear a pull-up, or for her to wet the bed?* I took a deep breath.

"Mom, just this once, since you can't get to the bathroom on your own, would you want to wear a pull-up? I mean, in case no one can help you right away."

"I don't care," she said, "I just want to go to bed."

I took that to mean she was willing.

"Do you have one?" I asked Renee.

She brought the padded underwear, and I helped Mom put it on.

Renee showed me how to work the bed. Then I wheeled Mom into the bathroom to brush her teeth. Like a four-year-old, she held the brush awkwardly, and brushed with jerky, ineffectual strokes. I did not step in to help. Instead, I thought maybe I should buy her an electric toothbrush.

It was a little after 7:00 P.M. when I tucked Mom into bed. I hugged her and kissed her cheek.

"Sleep tight," I said. "I'll be back early tomorrow, and I'll bring you some good coffee. I'll bet the coffee here is terrible." I smiled at her, but her eyes were closed.

"Thanks, honey. G'night."

I turned off the light over her bed, and pulled the curtain so Becky's light would not shine in her eyes. I said goodnight to Becky.

"I can bring you some coffee, too," I offered. "How do you like it?"

"You don't have to do that," she said. "But I like real cream. They only have the fake stuff here."

I walked down the gray hallway, now empty of wheelchairs, turned left at the nurses' station, and continued past the intake coordinator's office and out into the parking lot. I found my car and drove, without thinking, to the Harris Teeter for groceries. Klein called as I pulled into a parking space.

"I'm drained," I said. "She's at the nursing home. It's dismal. She's wearing a pull-up."

"What?"

"You know, those adult diapers that are like padded underpants. I mean, as a precaution, but I don't know, it's so…I don't know how we got here. I mean, I just didn't think we'd ever be here. I don't know."

"You sound tired. Are you okay?"

"No, but yes. I mean, I have to be okay. I have to figure out how to entertain her for the next few days—there's no TV. I cannot even imagine."

"How can there not be TV?"

"There's no TV in the rooms. I can get a TV, and they'll hook it up—but nothing until Monday."

"What about in a sitting room, or lounge, or something?"

"I didn't think of that. My mind is fried. I'll check tomorrow. Anyway, how are you?"

"I'm fine. Everything's good here. The kitties miss you."

"I miss them, too. And I miss you. But this is where I need to be."

"I know."

"I gotta go. I need to get some food and stretch out."

"Okay. Love you."

"Love you, too."

As I walked into Harris Teeter, I saw them turn off the lights in the prepared foods section, closing it down for the night.

No! No! I thought, and then came the tears.

Chapter 17

MY MELTDOWN IN THE GROCERY STORE CONFIRMED IT—five days into full-time caregiving, and I was a basket case. I cooked scrambled eggs for my dinner and sipped on red wine, thinking, *how does Barbara do it day after day? How can I expect her to continue doing it?* I was asleep by 9:00 P.M. and awake at 3:30 A.M., worrying about how to make the nursing home bearable. I lay in bed, dozing and planning, for an hour or so. Then I got up and got to work.

I typed up a one-page "introduction" to Mary Eleanor Pratt. Point number one was "She is called Eleanor." In other points, I lauded her intelligence: bachelor's degree in English, worked as a book editor and assistant to a doctor, elected president of both the hospital volunteers and the condominium association. I provided her backstory: grew up in Philadelphia, married to Dave for fifty-three years, raised her family of two girls in Northern Virginia near Washington, D.C., lived in Florida for thirty-five years, moved to New Bern two years ago, and lives at McCarthy Court. I listed some things she liked: all kinds of food, a nice glass of wine, cats and friendly dogs, a good joke, and, of course, television. I wanted them to see her as a human being, rather than just another old lady in rehab.

I selected a few books from Barbara's bookshelf, figuring if there was no TV, then I would read to Mom and Becky. I chose Julia Child's *My Life in France*, because Mom and I had enjoyed Julia's cooking shows over the years, and a collection of James Thurber stories that Mom often quoted with wild laughter.

I made a peanut butter sandwich for my lunch and headed out. I went to McCarthy Court and picked up some clothes for Mom. I chose three of her most colorful blouses, two pairs of slacks, underwear, and her favorite L'eggs knee-high stockings. Then I stopped on the way to Beechwood for my usual cappuccino and muffin, coffee for Mom and Becky, and some grapes for us all to snack on.

I arrived at around 7:30 A.M. and found both women dressed and sitting in their wheelchairs, pushed up to individual tables holding breakfast trays. Mom was eating scrambled eggs, and Becky was buttering some toast.

"Good morning," I sang.

They both looked up.

"Hi, honey," said Mom.

She didn't smile. I went over and hugged her, and she leaned into me for a moment. Then she went back to her breakfast.

"I brought coffee," I said. "With cream, for Becky. I put it in a separate cup so you can add as much as you like."

"Thank you so much." Becky reached for the cup I offered. "I'm still not hungry, but that coffee smells really good."

I chattered to both of them, telling them I had brought books and grapes, reviewing the weather—warm even this early in the day— and wondering aloud if we might go outside a bit today. I posted Mom's bullet-point biography on the bathroom door. Later in the day, I awarded myself an *attagirl* when one of the aides looked at the list and asked whether Mom wrote books.

As I hung Mom's clothes in the closet, I thought how she seemed to be fraying, just like the seams on her ancient lime green polyester stretch slacks. She was usually so social, but she wasn't even trying to engage Becky in conversation. She seemed distant and disconnected. I reminded myself that she needed time to recover from the physical trauma of the pacemaker surgery—and it had only been nine days since her big fall.

The rest of the day passed slowly. I played social director, trying to entertain my listless guests. Mom and I went exploring. I rolled her down the hall and we found the "living room" with its comfortable chairs, a large wood-and-glass aviary housing several colorful parakeets, and (hooray) a television. I told Mom we might come back later to watch TV. We found the dining room where rehab patients gathered for lunch and dinner. Three large windows filled the room with natural light. Four rectangular tables covered with faded flowered cloths offered space for six to eight people each. A staff member whose nametag read *Deanna* was setting up the tables for lunch. I greeted her by name, and introduced myself and Mom.

"When you come for meals, you can sit anywhere you want to," she said. "We'll bring you a tray. And we have sweet tea in a pitcher over there all day long, so you can get some anytime you want." She gestured to a small table in the corner.

"I only drink coffee," Mom stated.

"Well, we can bring you coffee with your meal," said Deanna. "I can even get you some now. Do you want some?"

"No, thanks," Mom said.

I thanked Deanna for her help.

"We just got here yesterday," I said, "so we're still learning how it all works."

"Okay, I'll see you at lunch," said Deanna.

I smiled at her and said thanks, again, trying to make up for Mom's lack of manners. Mom was so unlike herself, it scared me.

Back in the room, I chatted a bit with Becky. She lived at the Marriot Courtyards Senior Apartments in New Bern, formerly known as The Villages. That was the other option we had considered for Mom. Her daughter lived about twenty-five miles away and had two children, so she wouldn't be able to visit every day.

"She'll come by tomorrow after church," said Becky.

I read to Mom and Becky from the Julia Child book for about an hour or so. I didn't dare try the Thurber. If I read one of Mom's favorite passages and she didn't laugh, it would break my heart.

Around 11:30, the three of us trooped to the dining room for lunch. Becky nibbled on some rice, but Mom surprised me by eating nearly an entire chicken breast after I cut the meat off the bone. All the while, I talked with the man sitting next to Mom, though I remember nothing about him or our conversation. Mom seemed to be concentrating hard on her plate. She barely spoke.

After lunch, both Becky and Mom were ready for naps. I needed a break, and told Mom I would go home for lunch. I asked Becky if there was anything special she would like to eat. I suggested a milkshake, drawing on hospice lore that even very sick patients loved the cold creamy sweetness of a shake.

"That sounds good. Could I have chocolate?" she asked.

Instead of going home, I drove to a park and ate my sandwich outside. It was hot, but I wanted the sun and open air after the gloom of Beechwood. I forced myself to sit there for more than half an hour, and the whole time, I worried about what was happening at the home. There wasn't much I could do to improve the situation, but I felt it was my job to share her misery. On the way back, I stopped at McDonald's for Becky's milkshake, and stole a few sips for myself.

Mom and I watched some TV in the living room—the end of a *Law & Order* rerun, then *NCIS*. It turned out we had to ask someone at the nursing station anytime we wanted to change the channel. Mom dozed while I tried to lose myself in the mindless entertainment.

We went back to the room, and I read some more of the Julia Child book out loud. Mom and Becky had been granted permission for dinner in the room one more day. I kept listening for the clatter of serving trays, a sign that the day was finally winding down.

Once the food arrived, I helped the ladies organize their trays and open their cartons of protein drink. Then I went to the kitchen to get some hot coffee for Mom. As I wandered down an unfamiliar corridor, I saw a woman resident with a young man—her son or grandson, I supposed—watching a movie on a small DVD player. *Brilliant*, I thought.

"Hey, Mom," I said as I walked back into the room, "Barbara and Phil have a wonderful collection of movies and old TV shows on

DVD. What if I bring some of them in to watch tomorrow?" I figured I could get a reasonably-priced player at Walmart.

"I'd rather have a television," she said.

"I promise we'll get you a TV as soon as possible, but it won't be until Monday, at least."

"Okay. Will you still be here Monday?"

"Yes. I'll be here for another week or so." I was committed to staying as long as necessary, even after Barbara returned from vacation. I wondered what "necessary" might mean, or how long it might go on.

I took away the dinner trays, and helped Mom go to the bathroom, brush her teeth, and change into her nightgown. I rang the bell for an aide to get Mom tucked in. Renee came in about ten minutes later. She asked Mom about wearing a pull-up, and Mom agreed. It took me a minute to realize that the entire exchange had not involved me at all. That was good, right? It was good that Renee had addressed Mom directly, and good that Mom seemed comfortable with Renee. I could relax a little bit, couldn't I? Or could I?

I slept well that night, more likely from pure exhaustion than from any measure of relief. The knot in my stomach the next morning let me know I was still on high alert. I convinced myself to go to the gym—care for the caregiver. The voice in my head said *Mom will be okay.*

I left the gym at 7:00 A.M. and headed for Walmart (open twenty-four hours a day) to buy the DVD player. Then I went back to the house, showered, and drove over to Beechwood at around 9:30 A.M., stopping on the way to pick up some coffee for the ladies. I was proud of myself for honoring Mom's independence by going so late, and ashamed of myself for having left her alone for so long.

Mom was in the bathroom with Nelly, one of the aides, when I arrived. *See*, I told myself, *she does just fine without you.* I handed Becky some coffee and asked her how things were going.

"Okay. I ate some eggs this morning, and I'm feeling a little bit better." Hearing sad-sack Becky say something positive seemed like a good omen for the day.

I set up the DVD player, trying to put it in a place where both Mom and Becky could watch the tiny five-by-seven-inch screen. I showed Mom the DVD choices—*Breakfast at Tiffany's, Singin' in the Rain, Vertigo* (the Hitchcock classic), and the collection of old *Jack Benny* shows. She asked me what I wanted to see. I chose *Vertigo*.

"Jimmy Stewart and that elegant blonde," said Mom. "It's a good movie."

I smiled, happy she had recalled Jimmy Stewart's name and Kim Novak's cool beauty. About halfway through the movie, Becky's daughter, Susan, arrived. I hit the pause button.

After greetings and introductions, Susan thanked me for all I had done for Becky.

"It's no trouble," I said. "I'm here in New Bern just so I can look after Mom, and I'm staying at my sister's house, only fifteen minutes away."

After a bit more small talk, I suggested to Mom that we go down to the living room to watch TV. We caught up with Becky in the dining room at lunchtime. Susan had left, but would visit again in a few days, Becky told us.

My cell phone rang in the middle of lunch, and I was happy to see it was Barbara calling. We hadn't talked since Wednesday evening after Mom's pacemaker placement, though I had sent short email updates every day.

"How's it going?" Barbara asked.

"We're getting settled, I think. Mom still seems kind of removed, like from everything. Maybe that's a good thing." I had walked outside to take the call.

"We're thinking about coming back early, and not just because of Mom."

"Well, you don't have to come back for her. I'd rather you get your full away time. There'll be plenty to handle when you get back." I worried my emails had made her feel like she had to return, even though I had tried to keep them light.

"I know. But it would be nice to have some overlap time with you, so I can get up to speed quickly."

"Well, I'd love to get some time with you, too, but please stay away as long as you want to. I'm hoping Mom won't be here more than a week or so. I found some info in your files for the home rehab company. Do you have anything on home health agencies?"

"We've used Tar Heel Home Health. Check the accordion file next to the desk. Or you can call the nurse at Seniors Choosing, for a referral."

"Okay. I just want to start looking into options for when she goes home."

We talked a little about her trip. She and Phil had visited a friend in Portland, Maine, and then driven to Moncton, New Brunswick. She said it had rained for two days straight, but now it was beginning to clear.

"Tomorrow, we'll drive to St. John's and take the ferry to Nova Scotia. We'll spend the night, and then maybe head home. I'll keep you posted," she said.

"Do you want to say hi to Mom?"

"Sure."

I went inside and wheeled Mom into the corner near a window, then handed her the phone. She talked to Barbara for a few minutes. I heard her say, "Love you, too." I took back the phone, and told Barbara we'd talk again soon.

Back in Mom's room, I finished watching *Vertigo* while Mom and Becky dozed in their chairs. Then I put in the *Jack Benny* DVD. After five minutes or so, Mom asked me if we could change the channels. I explained that the player was not a television.

"But if you don't want to watch, we could read some more of the Julia Child book, or go for a walk."

"No, I'll watch this," said Mom, her voice still flat.

I excused myself and went into the bathroom. I washed my hands and splashed cold water on my face. Then I looked in the mirror and let out a huge sigh. I didn't want to be at Beechwood. I didn't want Mom to be there. I didn't want her to need to be there. I wanted to take her to a nice hotel and order room service, and let her change the channels to watch her favorite shows. I wanted to hear her laugh, or call out an answer—I mean a question—for a *Jeopardy* clue.

When I came out of the bathroom, a nurse was in the room talking to Becky. She looked over at me and I checked her name tag—Dorothy. I introduced myself, and she told me Becky would be moving to the rehab wing the next morning.

"That's great," I said. "Will someone else be moving in, or will Mom go to a new room, too?"

"I'm not sure," said Dorothy. "You could check with the administrator. She's not usually here on Sunday, but I just saw her. You might find her in her office."

I'd been eager to meet the administrator. It was part of my "make sure you know the people in power and they know you" strategy. I'd seen the sign designating her office in the entry hallway. She was on her way out when I walked up, but she graciously unlocked the door, flicked on the light, and invited me in.

After shuffling through a few papers on her desk, she said she had the request for a single room, and indicated that Mom would probably move to one on Monday or Tuesday. I asked a few more questions, and she confirmed that Mom would see the therapist the next day.

"She'll have several assessments—physical, memory, and occupational, meaning whether she can handle her activities of daily living by herself," she said.

I knew about the five activities of daily living (ADLs), because every hospice patient receives an ADL assessment to help determine which services they need. The names can change depending upon the institution, but the five are: bathing, dressing, transferring or ambulating (for example, walking and moving from bed to chair), toileting, and eating.

As I left the administrator's office, I felt hopeful. Tomorrow would be better. Mom would get her assessments, which was the first step toward getting her strong enough to go home. She might be moving to a better room. Dena would visit. And at last, I could put in my request for television service.

Chapter 18

As I walked into Beechwood on Monday, August 31, 2009, I wondered if Mom would remember it was her wedding anniversary—sixty-eight years since Mom and Daddy had married. She had been without him for fifteen years. When I got to her room, I forgot all about it.

Two aides—Nelly and one I hadn't seen before—were bustling around the room. Nelly was helping Mom get dressed, and the other aide was piling Becky's clothes onto a wheelchair and gathering her toiletries in a plastic tub. Becky looked up and smiled for the first time since we'd met.

"I'm moving to the rehab wing," she said, telling me the room number. I promised to visit her later that day.

"Miss Mary, I mean Miss Eleanor, is going to a new room later today," Nelly told me, "but right now, they want her down at the rehab room."

I asked if I should take her down there. Nelly said no, the therapist would come and get her. Just a few minutes later, Rose walked in and introduced herself. She sat on the bed and talked directly to Mom. I liked her immediately.

"In a few minutes, we'll go down to the rehab room and do some physical testing. Then later, probably after lunch, we'll check out your memory and a few other things," she said.

"I'm not walking very well, but I'll try," Mom said. I wanted to hug her.

"That's okay," said Rose, "It's our job to get you stronger. Shall we go?"

Mom nodded. I asked if I should come, and Rose said it would be better for me to wait in the room.

While they were gone, I went to find Becky. She greeted me warmly from a lovely upholstered chair with matching ottoman. I looked around her new room. Was I still at Beechwood? The sunny yellow walls looked freshly painted. The bed was made up with a colorful spread. On the facing wall stood a cherry wood veneer multipurpose unit—closet, small desk, three drawers, and an entertainment center, complete with flat screen television. I told Becky it looked like she had moved to rehab heaven.

"Isn't it nice?" she asked.

"Very different from the other wing," I said, nodding.

Now I wanted to know when and where Mom would be moving. I found the administrator.

"Your mother will move later today to a single room. It's still in the long-term care wing, right next to the nursing station," she told me.

The housekeeping staff was cleaning the new room when I stopped by to check it out. It was more spacious than her current room, but all that space looked extra drab now that I had seen the relative elegance of the rehab wing. It turned out the renovated rooms were first come, first served, and Becky had arrived an hour ahead of us. *Oh, well,* I thought, *at least Mom will still have the nurses and aides she is getting to know.* Anything that might ease her transition seemed like a plus considering all that she and I (and Barbara) had been through in the last ten days—her fall, eight days in the hospital, surgical placement of a pacemaker, and the move to Beechwood. No wonder she seemed a little shell-shocked. And no wonder I did, too.

As I came out of Mom's new room, I saw Rose pushing her in her wheelchair down the hall.

"How did it go?" I asked.

"I couldn't do very much," Mom said.

"You did just fine," said Rose. "We'll have to wait until we finish the assessment. Right now, I'm thinking we'll plan on about two weeks of rehab."

"That much, huh?" I said. Even after seeing her so weak, even after helping her to the bathroom, cutting her meat, and watching her hand tremble as she brushed her teeth, I hadn't quite absorbed the enormity of Mom's debility. Then I remembered that the rule of thumb for the elderly is a week of rehab for every day in the hospital—that would mean eight weeks for Mom! Now I wondered whether two weeks would be enough.

Nelly came and helped us move Mom to her new room.

"I like this room better," Mom said, "but where is the TV?"

"I promise I'll go get the TV this afternoon." *So predictable,* I thought, and smiled. I didn't tell her that it might take a few days to get it working.

While Mom went to lunch, I filled out the maintenance request form to get the television cable hooked up, and called the number I'd been given for the cable company. I set up an account for Mom, with the bills to come directly to me. I begged everyone to do whatever they could to make this a rush installation.

From then on, the week got better and better. The rest of the assessment confirmed the need for physical therapy to get Mom walking again with her walker, and occupational therapy focused upon trying to improve her cognition and memory. The care plan called for two hours of therapy per day for two weeks, and then reevaluation. I knew the nursing home had to have evidence that Mom could improve in order to get paid by Medicare, so I was hopeful she really would improve.

My pleas to the television gods were heard, and by Tuesday afternoon, Mom had access to her favorite shows. Also on Tuesday, Dena (whom Barbara and I had dubbed "our other sister") started to visit for two hours every day. She entertained Mom with chit-chat, took her outside in the wheelchair, and attended to the extra grooming Mom loved—trimming toenails, mini-manicures, and getting her hair washed at the Beechwood salon, a tiny room with a sink and hairdressing chair. It really seemed that having Dena back in her life on a regular basis made Mom feel more comfortable in her new surroundings.

Now I had lots more freedom. While Mom went to rehab, while she was with Dena, and while she was entertained by her shows, I could get some work done, spend an hour or so at the gym, or do errands. I used some of that time to look into options for care once Mom went back to her apartment at McCarthy Court. I wasn't at all sure how much help she would need, but I knew it would be more than she'd ever had before—maybe even twenty-four hours a day.

First, I contacted Valerie at Seniors Choosing to see if they offered round-the-clock care, and what it would cost. Then I set up a meeting with Diane at McCarthy Court. It was time to give her a detailed update on Mom, and get some information. I didn't even know whether McCarthy Court allowed residents who needed round-the-clock assistance.

Diane greeted me with a hug, and that simple expression of concern and support raised a lump in my throat. We pulled chairs up to the round table in her tiny office. I opened my "Mom Notebook" where I wrote down everything I needed to remember, and turned to the page where I had jotted down some questions.

Diane asked, "How's your mom doing?"

Suddenly, I was sobbing.

"Well, at the moment, not very well."

Diane pushed the tissue box toward me.

I apologized, and she said it was understandable.

"It just seems to be happening so fast," I said. "I know she'll get better, but I've never seen her so weak and listless."

As I calmed down, I filled Diane in on the pacemaker, the plan for at least two weeks of rehab, and our concern that Mom would need a lot more care once she returned home. It turned out there were people at McCarthy who had round-the-clock caregivers, and Diane had information on how to arrange the services. She said we should also consider assisted living at Homeplace. I reminded her that

Barbara and I had tried to convince Mom to move to Homeplace eight months ago, and it had been a fiasco.

"I remember," she said, "but a lot can change in eight months for someone like your mom."

She was so right. Mom was on the tail end of the growth and development curve. Between the ages of ninety-one and ninety-three, Mom had lost ground as quickly as a child gains skills and abilities between the ages of one and three. Mom wasn't "growing" old; she was wilting.

"Anyway," Diane continued, "We'll help you make the decision. I'll visit your mom at Beechwood. I always visit our residents when they are out for rehab. And I'll talk to the rehab staff there. Some of them also work at Homeplace. We'll all get together and recommend what we think would be best for your mother."

"So, is it possible that she would not be allowed to come back to McCarthy Court?"

"Well, it might be that we would require a certain level of supportive care to have her back here. What we can do is help you understand the options."

I was crying again. We had a lot to figure out, but we would have help.

Two days later, on Thursday afternoon, Barbara and Phil came home from vacation. I was flooded with relief. Was that how she felt whenever I showed up? If so, I needed to visit more often.

On Friday, Barbara and I arrived at Beechwood just as Mom was finishing up her morning rehab session. We found her walking down the hallway with her walker as the therapist held her up via a heavy, woven harness, and an aide following behind with a chair so she could stop to rest. That sad little parade made me so happy. She was walking—not well, and not much, but it looked good to me after only three days of therapy.

"I get pretty tired," Mom said when we were back in her room.

"That's okay. You're improving," I said.

I showed Barbara the room, the clothes I had brought over, and where the laundry basket was (since we'd agreed to do Mom's laundry at the house). I introduced her to Nelly, who had come to help Mom to the bathroom.

I told Barbara I'd show her how to help Mom on and off the toilet.

"You don't have to do it, but the aides aren't always available, so sometimes it's easier. You kind of get used to it," I said.

We had about an hour before lunchtime, so I suggested we go outside on the porch. It was hot, but shady, and Mom wanted to keep her sweater on. Barbara and I sat in rockers on either side of Mom, and Barbara talked about her trip—seeing her friend Dawn, the vast greenness of Nova Scotia, the sand dunes and spectacular seafood on Prince Edward Island. Mom listened and nodded, but still seemed distant. After a bit, she asked if it was time for lunch.

"I guess all the exercise makes you hungry, huh?" I joked.

"Yes, I guess it does," Mom said with the first little smile I had seen in over a week. She was getting better, and would get better still.

While Mom had lunch, I gave Barbara a tour of Beechwood— the dining room, where we dropped Mom off; the living room with the aviary; the renovated rehab wing that I had come to call "Oz" because it was so bedazzling after the grayness of the long-term care wings; the physical therapy/rehab room; and the nurses' station. Along the way, I introduced her to the therapists, nurses, and aides I knew.

"I will never be able to keep all those names in my head," Barbara said.

"Well, you don't have to, but it helps to know a few of them. It gets easier the more time you spend here."

"Do you think I need to come every day?"

"I did, at first. Then again, I don't have any other life here in New Bern. I think it's important to visit often, so everybody knows that Mom has someone watching over her. But with Dena coming and all, you probably don't have to come every day, and you certainly don't have to stay for hours and hours. Now, I just come late morning, and leave when Dena comes in the afternoon. Then I come back for an hour in the early evening."

I didn't know what, if anything, Barbara thought about my speech. What I thought was that I'd been spending way too much time at Beechwood. If Mom had lived near me, I would have given up my own life to tend to her. It was how I did things in general, and in this specific situation, it was my way of showing love and devotion.

Barbara was not neglectful—far from it. Before the big fall, she had been calling Mom every day, shopping for her, stopping by often, and managing the other caregivers. She slept with the phone by the bed, and worried each night that there might be a call to go to the emergency room. I had taken to calling her Saint Barbara. I found a picture of an ancient Saint Barbara, and sent it to her.

Barbara also lived her life. She kept some balance. She was able to disconnect.

"I don't really think about her as Mom anymore," she once told me. "I think of her as a little old lady who needs my help." Was that because Mom was so changed, or because it protected Barbara from some of the worry and heartache? I suspected it was little of both.

On Saturday, we visited Mom, and we also went to the movies and saw *Julie & Julia* with the incomparable Meryl Streep. That evening, we cooked lentil soup, and the next day, we brought some to Mom for lunch. She ate every bit, and asked for more.

After Sunday lunch, I drove back to Raleigh-Durham and flew to Cape Cod, where Klein and I had scheduled some vacation time. I didn't sleep on the plane, even though I was exhausted. Barbara had thanked me over and over for giving her much-needed time off. Her sincere gratitude just made me feel guilty for leaving her to continue doing what she had already been doing for two years, especially now that Mom's health had taken such a downward turn.

I ruminated on the events of the last two weeks. I understood the emotional strain, but I hadn't expected to feel so powerless. I had always believed that knowledge is power, and I had more knowledge about aging and the healthcare system than most people. I realized that my knowledge was abstract and academic—useful, but only in a limited way, because it was disconnected from real life. Now I was gaining experience. It was painful, potentially more useful, and still incomplete.

One question in particular nagged at me. Had the pacemaker made Mom better or worse? I had no confidence that I had made the right decision. I never would be sure.

Chapter 19

Aᴄᴏᴏʟᴇʀ, sunny days on Cape Cod. I caught up on work and sleep, all the while thinking I should have stayed in New Bern. Even though there was little I could do to help Mom, I was now acutely aware of everything Barbara had on her plate—a full-time job that required her to be at her home computer for much of the day while also keeping tabs on Mom, who would be needing more and more attention.

Just a few days after I left, Barbara took Mom to Dr. B.'s office for the follow-up appointment about the pacemaker. A medical technician did a chest X-ray to make sure the leads were positioned correctly, and an EKG to check overall heart function. Then Mom and Barbara met with a representative from the pacemaker company. She conducted a computer test to make sure the pacemaker was performing as expected, and gave Barbara the "other half" of the pacemaker—a device the size of a cell phone. This receiver was designed to sit next to Mom's bed and pick up signals from the implanted device. If a problem was detected, an email would go out to the doctor and to the pacemaker company's monitoring center.

"She wasn't scheduled to see Dr. B.," Barbara told me when we talked later that evening, "but I asked to meet him. He was very nice, but it was clear Mom did not remember him."

"Oh, well, he probably didn't remember her, either." Dr. B. would never get a fair shake from me. He was too wrapped up with my remorse about the pacemaker.

Barbara said she had planned to take Mom out for an early dinner, but had changed her mind, because Mom seemed so tired and confused.

"She kept asking me if I had her purse, if I had checked the mail, paid the bills. Then she apologized for being all at sixes and sevens, and asked where we were going. She asked, 'Where is home?'"

"Was she like that at the doctor's office?" I asked.

"Actually, she was pretty charming, like she always is with doctors."

"Maybe she felt confused because there was so much information. Complex discussions really upset her, and then she feels bad about it."

"All I know is, from the time I picked her up around 2:30 to the time I took her back, she really seemed to decline. I don't know if it was exhaustion, or what."

"It sounds like *sundowning*—it happens with Alzheimer's patients. They often get agitated or confused toward evening, as it gets dark outside; but Mom doesn't have Alzheimer's." I could feel my forehead wrinkling as I tried to puzzle out this new development.

"Anyway, I took her back to Beechwood and got her settled with one of her shows. Then I asked the nurse to let her have dinner in her room."

"Look, it always takes her a long time to bounce back from any trauma, and this was a big one. She probably just needs some time," I said.

"I know, but I don't have much optimism right now," Barbara replied. It was not what I wanted to hear.

Mom's confusion, combined with her minimal gain in strength from the physical therapy, turned out to be a recipe for danger. Now she could stand up on her own, but she didn't remember that she couldn't walk without help. She'd get up from her chair or bed to go the bathroom, and promptly half-fall, half-sit on the ground.

Barbara talked to Geneva, the night nurse at Beechwood, to see if Mom was using the call button and not getting a response.

"Geneva said Mom thinks she can get around by herself. Although one time Mom claimed to have pushed the call button, and it turned out she was pushing the TV remote control," Barbara told me. "They're going to put an alarm on her bed and her wheelchair. It makes a terrible noise if she gets up, so it reminds her to sit down, and also alerts the staff that she needs help."

"Ugh. It sounds like Pavlov's dogs. I guess if it keeps her from falling, I'm okay with it," I said. "I feel like this is our life now—finding ways to keep Mom upright."

"The good news is that Geneva and the other nurses think Mom is an absolute dear," Barbara added.

We agreed that Mom would need twenty-four-hour care once she left Beechwood, and we discussed the options: let her go back to McCarthy Court and get round-the-clock caregivers, or convince her to move into assisted living at Homeplace.

Barbara told me she had recently reminded Mom about Homeplace.

"She quickly protested that she'd have to live in only one room," Barbara said. "Even with her raisin brain, she remembers that!"

"I really hate this," I said. "Maybe it will come down to the rehab people: Diane at McCarthy, and the nurse at Homeplace. Maybe they'll take the decision out of our hands. Plus, I would think Dr. S. will weigh in when the times comes."

"The thing is, I'm not even sure what Mom can afford."

"I'll work on that," I said. "I got some of the costs for private caregivers when I was there, and I have info for Seniors Choosing. I'll call Homeplace and get a list of prices, then do a comparison," I said. My left brain perked up at having a concrete task that would be helpful.

When I talked to Kathy, the director at Homeplace, she reminded me that "assisted living" isn't, in fact, very assisted at all. Though there are staff on duty all the time, and three meals a day are served in the dining room, residents have to get themselves dressed and down to the dining room on their own.

"You can buy 'extra-care points' if your Mom needs help with dressing or medication, but if she needs twenty-four-hour care, you would have to pay for that privately," Kathy explained.

I built an Excel spreadsheet comparing the cost of McCarthy Court, a double room at Homeplace, and a single room at Homeplace, plus various add-ons (Dena, the additional "care points" available at Homeplace, more help from Seniors Choosing, and private caregivers) to give Mom round-the-clock coverage. Factoring in the additional caregivers took her monthly costs from her current level of about $3000 per month to as much as $15,000 per month in a private room at Homeplace. Since the base price at McCarthy was much less than Homeplace, it made financial sense for Mom to stay in her apartment if she needed total care.

Barbara sent daily—and often twice daily—updates:
Mom walked the length of the hallway from rehab to the nurses' station and back, but Kristin (the therapist) steered her and supported her the whole way with the big belt, and she stopped two times to rest. They want her to stay three more weeks!

Even when Mom is confused about her own situation, she still knows who the president is and who I am; it just seems to come and go.

I saw Mom right after lunch. I borrowed a walker from rehab, and she walked almost as well as she used to, which means slowly and erratically—but anyway, better than yesterday. She asked me when she could get out.

Dena called me this morning to report on her visit with Mom yesterday afternoon. Mom was more "down"—she really fades in the late afternoon/early evening.

I talked to one of the therapists who fills in on Saturday. She didn't know Mom, but pulled her chart and told me her "mental scores" are 50% to 60%. I don't know what that means, but they want her to be around 80%.

All the references to Mom's mental state unnerved me. I Googled "stages of dementia" and sent one of the many lists I found to Barbara.

"I'm trying to get used to the idea that Mom is really getting worse mentally," I wrote.

Barbara sent back the list with her comments typed in italics. Her assessment was *Stage 1: Early difficulties.* That didn't sound so bad to me. I wasn't ready to think about the fact that dementia is almost always progressive. And I wasn't ready to think about the new option for Mom's care that presented itself a few days later.

"I saw Rose today. She's the rehab therapist who also works weekends at Homeplace," Barbara said the next time we were on the phone. "She suggested we consider Seasons, the memory unit at Homeplace, for Mom."

"No way," I said. "That's for Alzheimer's patients. Mom would be having dinner with a bunch of zombies. Anyway, it's just over a month since her fall. She'll bounce back. You'll see."

"Mel, she's already had almost three weeks of intense therapy. I think we have to be realistic."

What was she saying? Mom was still "with it" in so many ways. But then again, she did need the alarm on her bed. My cheeks were tingling, and my eyes felt hot.

"Mel?" Barbara said. "Mel?"

"Yes, I'm here."

"Look, let me find out more about it. I'm going over there to see what's available at Homeplace, and I'll get more information about Seasons, too."

"Okay. I guess that makes sense. Get some cost info, and I'll add it to the spreadsheet." I must have sounded as defeated as I felt.

"I'm sorry," Barbara said. "The thing is, I can see how much she's declined. She might get better, but she might not."

"I know," I said. "I just don't want to know."

There are four main stages of dementia. It should be noted that the stages of dementia can progress at different rates, and carers should not see initial symptoms as predictors of end stage incapacity.

Stage 1 - Early Difficulties

May be characterized by the following symptoms:

Forgetfulness - *YES*

Reduction of attention span - *YES*

Lack of spontaneity - *SOMETIMES*

Lack of initiative - *YES*

Disorientation of time and place - *SOMETIMES*

Depression and fear - *NOT MUCH*

Anxiety or suspiciousness about possessions, or about the behavior of other people - *NO*

Stage 2 - Emergence of Significant Difficulties

May be characterized by the following symptoms:

Problems recognizing close family and friends - *NO*

Difficulties dealing with money – *SHE JUST DOESN'T. WE DO IT.*

Restlessness and agitation - *NO*

Repetitiveness in conversation and actions – *YES, BUT MAY BE DUE TO FORGETFULNESS*

Increased disorientation and forgetfulness - *SOME*

Stage 3 - Confirmation of Diagnosis

NONE OF THESE, EXCEPT ONE?

May be characterized by the following symptoms:

Uncharacteristic mood swings and outbursts

Speech impediments

Wandering around home and away from home

Impaired judgment – *YES, SOMETIMES*

Increased disorientation of time and place

Stage 4 - Dependency and Incapacity

NONE OF THESE, EXCEPT SHE DOES NEED ASSISTANCE WITH DAILY LIVING BECAUSE OF PHYSICAL LIMITATIONS

Assistance with all the activities of daily living (washing, dressing, feeding)

The person may no longer talk

The person may no longer recognize family members

Inability to make decisions

Coexistence of other medical and physical conditions

This is the list of stages of dementia I sent to Barbara, with her comments added in italicized capital letters. This is just one of many similar staging systems.

Over the next week, Seasons rose to first place on the list of possibilities for Mom's next home. The ten Seasons rooms, all the same size as the "regular" assisted-living rooms in Homeplace, were arrayed on one hall that was separated from the rest of the facility by a locked door. Entry to Seasons was controlled by a big red push button on the wall. Exit from the locked section required keying a code into a number pad. Though the Seasons residents had their own shared living room and dining room, they could participate in all the Homeplace activities, including field trips. *Okay, she won't be too isolated,* I thought.

A Seasons room cost more than a Homeplace room, and for good reason. Like many memory care units, it came with a lot more services. What made it particularly attractive was the twenty-four-hour nursing station and the certified nursing assistants. Mom would have help dressing and taking her medications. The staff would check on her frequently, even at night, so while we would still want to have Dena visit, we might not need to hire any other additional caregivers. Barbara met with Kathy, the director of Homeplace and Seasons, toured both sections, and talked to some of the staff and residents. The next time she and I were on the phone, she sounded almost giddy.

"I'm telling you, Seasons was a lot more lively than McCarthy. I guess it's because the residents don't tend to stay in their rooms. Anyway, Kathy showed me a single room that's available now. I think it could be perfect," Barbara cooed.

"Can Mom roam over to Homeplace by herself, if she can remember the code?"

"I don't know. Probably not, but the Seasons residents go over there for activities every day."

"What about the people? Are they fairly sharp, like Mom? I don't want her to feel like that guy in *One Flew Over the Cuckoo's Nest.*"

"Mel, it's not an insane asylum. Anyway, I walked around, and the residents seem a lot like Mom, and they looked good. I mean, they were well-groomed, not unkempt. One of them is a former French teacher, and sang *Happy Birthday* to one of the aides in French.

Kathy said the woman is often very sharp, except, of course, when she's not."

"Sounds like Mom, I guess. What's our next step?"

"I put Mom's name on the list for both Seasons and regular Homeplace. There's nothing available at Homeplace right now, which is another reason I like the Seasons option. Kathy will call me if anyone else expresses an interest in the single room in Seasons."

I hung up and checked the clock. Not quite 5:00, but I was ready for a glass of wine. I poured some Chardonnay, grabbed a sweater, and headed for the back porch. September was my favorite month on Cape Cod. The cool mornings warmed up quickly, and the afternoon sun reflected bright greens and golds off the trees across our backyard pond. I stared at those trees, knowing I had just rained on Barbara's parade. She had said Seasons was perfect, and I tried my best to shoot holes in the plan. She deserved better. In fact, if I were honest, she probably knew better—what was better for Mom. What were my motives? Was I trying to protect Mom? From what? From dementia? From being old? Or was I trying to protect myself from facing the magnitude of Mom's decline?

Here I was, a recognized expert in quality of life at the end of life, and a daughter who had vowed to give her mother the best life possible until she died. So, what was quality of life for Mom? Above all, she prized her independence. She'd said it over and over again: "I just don't want to be a burden." Anything that made her less of a burden on Barbara was good. At Seasons, Mom could have her own space with 24-hour care nearby, but no one would be "living with her." And at Seasons, she'd be encouraged to participate in activities every day, whereas at McCarthy, she'd be left alone in her apartment.

I felt like it was too soon for Mom to go to Seasons. She still had most of her faculties. On the other hand, I could see how current circumstances made this a good time for the move. So often, with older parents, it seems like it's too soon for the next step—like you have a little more time—until suddenly, it's too late. Maybe, for once, we would beat the clock.

I went to my desk and wrote an email to Barbara, telling her that Seasons was probably a good idea.

It reminds me of when Mom would buy our shoes or clothes a little larger, so we could wear them for a longer time. I feel like Mom has one more move in her, but only one, so maybe we should get her something she can grow into. This is really hard.

It fell to Barbara to broach the subject of Homeplace—actually, Seasons—with Mom. She told me she watched for openings, then snuck up on the topic a little at a time. When Mom mentioned, as she did almost every day, how much she liked getting three meals a day at Beechwood, Barbara said she could still have all three meals if she moved to Seasons. Mom didn't jump at it, but said she knew she might "have to make some changes." That was serious progress.

The next day, Mom said something about how much she appreciated the extra help she was getting at Beechwood, and from Barbara and Dena. Barbara took up that thread, explaining to Mom that the rehab therapists felt she would need to have a lot more care when she returned home, probably someone living with her full-time.

"You mean someone like Dena?" Mom asked.

"Yes, but it wouldn't be Dena. Of course, if you moved to Seasons, you would have a lot more privacy, because you would have your own room," Barbara said. I marveled at how she emphasized what Mom would get at Seasons, rather than what she might be giving up at McCarthy.

"So, has she actually agreed?" I asked Barbara the next time we were on the phone.

"No, but she's not really protesting anymore. The thing is, we need to make a decision. It's almost the end of September, and if she moves out before the end of the month, she can stop paying for the McCarthy apartment."

"You think we can just take her straight to Seasons from Beechwood?"

"Truly, I think that would be best. I think it might help her adjust to Seasons more quickly. She's been out of her apartment for six weeks now, and she's asked me more than once where she lives."

"What do you say when she asks?"

"I say that for now she is staying at Beechwood. I avoid naming any place as 'home.'"

"I am promoting you to Senior Saint," I proclaimed. "I wouldn't know what to say. It makes me want to cry."

Barbara and I agreed that we needed to get all the right people on board—the rehab staff, Diane at McCarthy, Kathy at Homeplace/Seasons—and then present the move to Seasons as "what everyone agrees is best." It turned out they had already talked, and were way ahead of us, worried that we would need to be convinced.

"I'm so relieved," Diane said. "Kathy and I really feel your Mom will do well at Seasons—much better than coming back to McCarthy."

I was finally beginning to see the pattern. After an illness or injury, Mom would lose ground both mentally and physically. Over time, she would regain some, but not all, of the lost territory. At each new and lower plateau, the space around her contracted, and Barbara and I would weed out what no longer fit.

Barbara signed all the papers, wrote the check for the deposit, and measured the room at Seasons. She sent me a proposed layout for some of Mom's furniture, and included a new single bed—the double bed we had bought for McCarthy Court was now too big.

I stared at Mom's downsized life. It seemed small and eminently manageable. It contained exactly what she would need to feel at home—her bed table and lamp; her bureau with the little gold tray on top that held her perfume; her two favorite living room chairs and the small round coffee table; the entertainment console where we would place her new flat screen TV; and her beloved glass étagère. I still had the picture showing exactly how to arrange the items on each shelf.

Chapter 20

I MADE PLANS TO GO TO NEW BERN for the first weekend in October to help set up Mom's room at Seasons, then sort through all the remaining things in her McCarthy Court apartment. I sandwiched my visit between the National Hospice and Palliative Care Clinical Team Conference in Denver and the Alabama Hospice Organization meeting in Montgomery. Ironically, I was presenting lectures on managing hospice quality of care, and simultaneously struggling to figure out what was best for my own mother.

I arrived Thursday evening, and Barbara and I drove over to visit Mom at Beechwood at around 7:00 P.M. She was sitting up in bed, snacking on some graham crackers.

"You look like a queen," I said, giving her a hug.

"I feel like a queen, especially now that you're here." Mom smiled. I had not seen that smile in a long time, and it stopped my heart.

I sat at the end of the bed, pulling up my knees and leaning on my elbow near Mom's feet. Barbara muted the television and we chatted about my trip, Mom's rehab, and the weather. Then Mom asked if I'd be back tomorrow.

"Of course, I'll come for a visit, but most of the day, Barbara and I will be moving your things into your new place at Seasons." I said it as if it were completely normal, and not the upheaval it felt like.

Mom's smile faded.

"So, it's all decided?" she asked.

She had been told about the move several times. Barbara had told her. I had talked to her about it by telephone. We knew it hadn't sunk in, and we were pretty sure it wouldn't until she was there.

"Yes," I said.

"Whether I want it or not?"

"Mom, everyone agrees—Dr. S., especially. This is what you need right now." I knew how she valued the doctor's advice.

"It's gonna be okay," Barbara reassured her.

I hugged Mom's legs.

"Will you stay for *Jeopardy*?" Mom asked.

"But of course," I said, hugging her again.

Barbara and I skipped a walk the next morning. The move would provide our exercise for the day. Kathy had given Barbara the code for the back door at Seasons, and shown her where they kept the big rolling cart we could use to ferry things across the parking lot from McCarthy.

Phil helped us move the furniture, including the glass étagère and its contents. Then Barbara and I chose the smaller items, with an eye toward making Mom's room at Seasons feel as much like home as possible. We took the artwork from the walls that faced her favorite chair. We took the pastel portrait of the two of us sitting on the piano bench in our party dresses at ages four (me) and eight (Barbara). We took the crewel-work cat picture Mom had stitched, a favorite afghan, everything from the top of her bureau, and those damned cat sheets, even though they were too big for her single bed. We took the cracked grape-cluster pitcher she liked to have in the bathroom.

By Saturday afternoon, the room at Seasons was full of personality. The only institutional item was the small white board hung next to the closet. Barbara said it was used to remind residents of the day and date, and to leave messages for the staff if residents had something special scheduled, like a doctor's appointment or dinner with family.

I looked around the room.

"Amazing," I said. "It almost looks as if Mom already lives here."

"Technically, she does," Barbara replied.

"God, I hope she likes it." I smoothed a few wrinkles out of the bedspread.

"Either way, I think we did a good job. It really looks nice."

We transferred the phone and the cable television account. All that remained was to bring Mom and the new television over from Beechwood. She was due to be sprung sometime in the following week, so Barbara would be the one to escort the queen to her new palace.

"Call me the minute you know what day she's moving in," I said. "I'll send a plant to welcome her."

Barbara and I spent that evening and Sunday morning sorting through the rest of Mom's stuff. I hated discarding parts of Mom's life as if they had no worth. I convinced myself I could use many of Mom's things at my house, even though I had not yet unpacked all the boxes I'd brought home to Miami from her condo two years earlier. I filled Daddy's Vermont Academy trunk full of pots and pans, other kitchenware, and Mom's collection of Beatrix Potter figurines—Peter Rabbit, Jemima Puddleduck, Benjamin Bunny, Mrs. Tiggy-Winkle—and addressed the trunk to Florida. I convinced Barbara to take several small furniture pieces to hold for me until I could arrange to ship them.

Barbara was more practical. She chose only a few items—the huge Chinese porcelain bowl that Great Uncle Homer had brought back from the Far East, a small side table she needed for her guest room, and a framed photograph of Mom as a young woman. The filing cabinet with Mom's paperwork also went to Barbara's house, minus the files I would need to work on Mom's taxes next April.

Barbara called Habitat for Humanity on Monday to donate the rest of the furniture. The following week, she saw Mom's living room in the window of the ReStore. The week after that, it had gone to a new home.

Mom moved into Seasons on Wednesday, October 7, 2009. She told Barbara, "It looks nice." Then she asked, "Is this where I live now?"

Mom asked what had happened to her apartment, and all her other things. Barbara explained, and then I explained again when I talked to Mom on the phone the next day. She told me everyone at Seasons was very nice, but she still hoped she could go back to her apartment someday. Two days later, she was back in the hospital.

On her second morning at Seasons, Mom got out of bed early and fell flat on her face. Because of cuts on her forehead that needed stitches, the Seasons staff called an ambulance. Barbara and Phil met her in the emergency room, and, as usual, she said she was fine, and didn't have any pain at all. The medical record described her as "pleasantly demented," and noted that she knew her name and where she was, but not the day, month, or year.

"They did a CAT scan of her brain and saw a subdural hematoma, meaning some bleeding between the brain and the thin membrane that covers it," Barbara told me. "But the bleeding may or may not have been caused by her fall, and could easily have been there since an earlier fall."

"Was she dizzy or lightheaded?" I asked.

"Nope, she seemed fine. The ER doctor offered to send her to the trauma center, where they might decide to treat the bleed surgically, but I told them not to. I told them we did not want any aggressive treatments, and definitely no surgery."

"Good. That's what Mom wants—or doesn't want, I mean. So, is she back at Seasons?" I asked.

"No, they admitted her for observation, maybe a day or two. I'm not worried," Barbara said.

"I just don't know what to do about this constant falling," I moaned.

I cursed the doctors who had convinced me to implant that pacemaker. I couldn't see that it was doing her any good, at least in terms of her falls, and I was afraid the surgery had accelerated her decline. I blamed myself. This did not seem like the best life possible for Mom.

Barbara said that Letty, the head nurse at Seasons, had been very apologetic, and promised they would watch Mom more closely.

"But as we know, she can fall even when someone is right beside her," I replied.

Two days later, Mom was back at Seasons, and she told Barbara it was good to be home.

"Home? That sounds good," I said.

"Yeah, maybe that little trip to the hospital had some weird effect, because she seems to be taking to Seasons now," Barbara said, filling me in. "She looks horrible—scabs on her nose and forehead, and two black eyes. But she barely remembers the fall, and is constantly surprised when people ask her what happened." Barbara chuckled. "It's actually pretty funny."

I called Mom every other day, and it usually took two or three tries before I reached her. An email from Barbara explained that Mom was staying busy.

The other day, I ran into Madeleine, the activities director at Homeplace. She said that Mom has been participating in everything for several days—even bingo! They're having happy hour today. Do you suppose they actually serve liquor? It sort of scares me, but mostly I think, "What the heck?!"

All in all, it seemed like Mom was less aware of everything, including her own decline and shortcomings. She was better for it, and I was grateful—finally, a good side to her worsening dementia.

Barbara also sent great stories about the reemergence of Mom's sense of humor and sociability. Dena was with Mom at dinner one day, sitting next to a man who used to be a preacher. He asked Mom if she wanted to go to heaven, and she replied that she'd rather be in hell with her friends, smiled, and then said she didn't believe in heaven or hell. The preacher said he'd never met anyone who felt that way. "Well, now you have," Mom said. Barbara said she felt bad for the preacher, except she was pretty sure he forgot all about it in a matter of minutes.

A few days later, Barbara went to Seasons to pick up Mom and take her to see Hamp for a haircut. Both Barb and Mom had been going to Hamp's shop for years. Mom had forgotten all about her haircut. She was out with the gang having lunch at Paula's Pizza, and barely got back in time for her appointment.

During her haircut, I asked Mom whether she had enjoyed her lunch, Barbara wrote. *She told me it was not a good place to go for Chinese food. I told her that made sense, because it was a pizza place. "Oops, slip of the mind," she said, and laughed. Later, Hamp told Mom she must have been a firecracker when she was younger. She said, "Depends on who I was firing at."* Barbara wrote that she laughed herself to tears.

The Seasons staff really stepped up their game with Mom, checking on her every thirty minutes, all day and all night. Whenever possible, they stationed an aide in her room at night to make sure she would not get out of bed by herself. We also started asking about a bed alarm, or a hospital bed with railings they could raise at night. The nurses seemed to think that either one would violate restrictions on the use of "restraints." Nursing homes had been subject to penalties (based on state inspections) for overuse of restraints, the implication being that they were using either medication (chemical restraint) or physical restraints rather than more staff-intensive ways of controlling patients who were disruptive or tended to roam. In this case, we wanted the restraints, and felt they would improve Mom's safety. We took our request to Kathy, the director. She said they preferred not to use hospital beds or alarms.

Through October and November, Mom fell a few times, but with no serious injury. Since every medical record indicated osteoporosis, it seemed miraculous that she never broke any bones. Letty told us the policy at Seasons was not to send residents to the hospital unless they were severely hurt or needed stitches. They understood how distressing it was for everyone to spend time in the emergency room.

Since the falls happened mostly at night or early in the morning, we asked again about getting a bed alarm or a hospital bed. We were told it was not permitted, with another vague reference to regulations.

Klein and I visited for Thanksgiving. We rented a PT Cruiser because the seats were level with Mom's hips, and easier for her to get into and out of than a model with bucket seats. Barbara made a traditional feast with all the trimmings. I cut Mom's turkey for her, but she fed herself, and ate a huge slice of mince pie for dessert. By 7:00 P.M., she was tired.

Barbara and I took her back to Seasons, leaving the husbands to clean up the kitchen. As soon as we got to Mom's room, Letty came to say that an aide would be in shortly to help Mom get ready for bed.

"We'll do it," I said.

"No, you girls go ahead and visit. I'll see you tomorrow," said Mom.

"Melanie and Klein are coming to take you out to lunch tomorrow," Barbara said as she wrote FRIDAY – Lunch with Melanie and Klein on Mom's white board.

Barbara and I hugged her. It had been a good day.

The next day, Klein and I drove over to Seasons to take Mom to lunch and for a drive around the marina nearby. When we arrived around 11:30, Mom's room was empty. The aide told us she was in the activities room. We found her sitting in her wheelchair at the head of the table, playing bingo with about forty other residents. Her card looked pretty full, but no bingo yet. She said a quick hello to Klein and me.

"Ready for lunch?" I asked.

"Not yet," she said, "I want to finish my game."

At first, I was annoyed, but I quickly realized how good it was that she preferred living her life to leaving it for lunch with us. That was the best it could be. And after the game, we went out into a cold but sunny day, and enjoyed a lunch of hamburgers and french fries.

During the Thanksgiving trip, Barbara and I congratulated ourselves on pulling off the move to Seasons. Mom seemed happy. When she had lived at McCarthy Court, she had stayed in the apartment and watched television all day. At Seasons, she was active. She told Barbara, "I don't like to just sit and suck my thumb. If I get an opportunity to get up and go, I'm going." That sounded like my good old mother! Moreover, the Seasons staff found her delightful.

"She makes us all laugh," Letty told me. "We keep her near the nursing station for much of the day so we can keep an eye on her. Sometimes, she still tries to get up, but we stop her, and then we scold her. She just smiles and says she forgot again."

In early December, Homeplace put on a Christmas pageant. Mom practiced for days with the other members of the choir. On the day of the pageant, all the participants sported Santa hats, elf hats with ears, or antlers. Barbara and Dena sat in the audience and waved to Mom.

Mom grinned the whole time, except when she had to look down at her music sheet to find the words to the songs, Barbara wrote in an email. *It definitely reminded me of our school pageants, and I mean the lower grades! It was wonderful.*

A week later, Mom fell again. She tried to get out of bed at around 9:45 P.M., fifteen minutes after she had been checked on. She bumped her head pretty hard, and needed stitches for a cut on her arm.

"I yelled for help," Mom told Barbara, "and they came right away."

The night nurse had called an ambulance, then called Barbara. She and Phil met Mom at the emergency room.

Barbara told the ER doctor that Mom really could not walk without assistance. "But she doesn't believe it," Barbara explained, "so she has already fallen at least three times this month."

"I feel like I should just tape one of the discussions with these ER docs," Barbara told me on the phone when she called from the hospital. "I could play it the next time Mom is brought in."

"It's always the same," she continued. "Mom denies any pain— well, actually, this time, she says the back of her head hurts, and she does have a big goose egg there. The doctor always says she's in good shape for a ninety-three year old; she's not dizzy or lightheaded. They do a CAT scan and report on her brain bruise (the subdural hematoma), which is actually getting smaller. And she always needs something minor—stitches, or whatever. This time, it's stitches."

"And her skin is really thin, so it's hard to stitch up, right?" I added.

"Yep."

"I guess you're pretty tired of it all."

"Yep."

"I really think we have to raise the issue of the bed alarm again. This is getting ridiculous. I'm going to call Kathy tomorrow," I said.

"Okay. I'm too tired to think about it right now. Phil's here. He always insists on coming with me for these night runs. We'll wait for her to get stitches, and then for an ambulance to transport her back. It's just too hard to get her into the car."

The next day, Barbara wrote to report on the end of the evening.

Somewhere around 1:30 A.M., as the EMTs were wheeling Mom's gurney back in the front door at Homeplace, she merrily sang out "I'm alright, I can walk from here." I thought I would die laughing—right after I punched her lights out.

Oh, my God, I wrote back. *You're channeling her sense of humor. I need to get up there and give you a break!*

Barbara and Phil had planned to get away for a few days the following week, when they would drive to Northern Virginia to visit with Phil's son and his girlfriend over the Christmas holidays. Before she left, Barbara got permission for a wheelchair alarm. Letty thought that would work better than a bed alarm for training Mom not to get up on her own.

The alarm looked like a large heating pad, and sat under Mom's wheelchair seat pillow; the electric cord wrapped around the chair leg and plugged into the nearest outlet. Barbara had bought the alarm at the medical supply store, and delivered it to Seasons a few days before her trip. Letty had told her to go and have a wonderful time. They would take good care of Mom.

On Christmas Eve, I called Mom when I knew she was with Dena. I had sent a card and her favorite pears from Harry and David, my go-to source for gifts of fresh fruit and snacks. We reminisced about Christmas Eves when Barbara and I were growing up. We always decorated the tree, and then our good friends the Zayannis would come over for cookies and Mom's homemade eggnog.

"Dena brought me some eggnog," Mom said.

"I'll bet it's not as good as yours was," I teased.

"Yeah, no rum," she replied, and I laughed.

I reminded Mom that I'd be visiting in just under a month to celebrate her birthday.

"Oh, good. We can have a hug," she said.

I emailed Barbara and told her that Mom seemed to be doing great.

The next day, Christmas afternoon, Mom left an angry message on Barbara's voicemail.

"Barbara, call me right away. I'm being held prisoner."

Mom with the delightful Dena at Homeplace on December 31, 2009. Photo taken by Homeplace staff.

Chapter 21

"MOM IS NOT HAPPY," Barbara told me about a week before the new year began. "The Seasons staff is keeping her in the common areas so they can watch her constantly. She still doesn't remember that she can't walk, so she tries to get up and the alarm blasts her back in her seat."

"Why is it so loud?" I asked.

"Because Mom's hearing is so bad, and getting worse," Barbara groaned.

"Well, I'll be there in a couple of weeks. I have some meetings at Duke, in Durham, and then I'll drive down to New Bern for several days."

"It'll be good to see you. Meanwhile, I sent a message to Valerie at Seniors Choosing. I want to get more hours with Dena. When she's there, Mom can stay in her room, and the two of them get along great. I go over almost every day, but I can't stay long. I have to work. And I can't stand to be there, doing not much at all, hour after hour."

"There's no reason you should," I said. "Get Dena to go. And I'll hang out with her when I'm there, too."

For a week or more, Mom's bad mood escalated. Barbara wrote that Mom seemed somewhat depressed, but mostly just angry. Mom complained she was being punished unjustly. She hadn't done anything wrong, but was forced to sit near the front desk. I called to see if I could calm her down.

"I don't get it," Mom said. "Why can't I get up and walk around when I want to?"

"Because your balance is no good, and you fall," I said.

"I haven't fallen in ages," she said, confirming what Barbara had told me. Mom had no memory of her falls.

"Yes, Mom, you do fall, and even get hurt. Look in the mirror. We're just trying to keep you safe," I said.

"That doesn't cut it," she snapped.

I tried to change the subject, telling her I was looking forward to my trip.

"Well, I hope you can take care of this when you're here."

I told her I would do my best.

Barbara recounted similar conversations with Mom.

"I explained that the alarm and sitting near the desk are for her protection. She gave me the stink eye and said, 'So you say.'"

"Jeez, I guess this could be worsening of her dementia. People with dementia can get really nasty and combative. Is it that bad, do you think?" I asked.

"I don't know. She's plain old pissed. I really can't blame her, but it's hard to see her feeling so low after things were good for so long."

Barbara said they were due to see Dr. S. in a few days. She planned to ask him about upping her antidepressant, or maybe even prescribing something else.

Suddenly, my hospice work brain slipped into gear. "Oh, wait!" I exclaimed. "Have him check for a urinary tract infection (UTI). I just remembered they can be weird in older people—none of the usual symptoms, but often a change in mood."

A few days later, Barbara wrote that Mom was much better—*all the way back from Mr. Hyde to Dr. Jekyll*. Dr. S. had increased her Lexapro antidepressant, but it was too soon to be seeing any effect. I wondered if this was the beginning of a series of mood swings.

When we next spoke by phone, Barbara recounted a conversation with Mom about her upcoming ninety-fourth birthday.

"Don't take this wrong," Mom had said to Barbara, "but I am ready to go anytime, and I hope it happens when I'm asleep."

"I hope she gets her wish," I said.

"I agree," Barbara replied. "I told her I was glad she was getting such good care in the meantime, and she said she liked Seasons very much, and liked having all her beautiful things around her."

It was everything I needed to hear at that moment—like a ray of sun poking through gray clouds.

"Every time the phone rings, I think it might be you calling to tell me she's gone," I said. "But then I talk to her, and it seems it could be a long time."

"Yeah, I wish we could know how long she has."

"Not in our hands," I replied.

Barbara made arrangements to throw a party for Mom's birthday on January 16, 2010. She reserved the private dining room at Homeplace and invited the Seasons staff, Dena, Jamie (who filled in on Dena's day off), Sophie, a few other friends from McCarthy Court, and Hamp, the hairdresser. She bought birthday plates, napkins, and party hats, and baked Mom's favorite sour-milk chocolate cake.

The night before the party, Mom fell. She hit her head, and opened a large cut over her left eyebrow. She and Barbara met at the usual place—the Carolina East Medical Center emergency room—and went through the usual song and dance. Mom denied any pain, and made the doctor laugh by asking, "Am I going to make it?" Barbara declined a CT scan, making it clear that Mom wanted comfort measures only. When pressed by the doctor, who was concerned they might miss something, she told him to look up the records of Mom's previous subdural hematoma and the decision not to treat it.

"Even if you find something, we will not want treatment," Barbara told the doctor.

He numbed Mom's forehead, and used nine stitches to close the v-shaped wound.

The medical record for that night described the usual healthcare system response to any fall with a face laceration—recommendation for a CT scan and for follow-up with plastic surgery to minimize scarring. It fell to Barbara to calmly rein the doctors in more than once with reminders about Mom's age, her mental and physical decline, and her personal choice to have comfort measures only.

The photos from the birthday party show Mom sporting a big white bandage and a spreading bruise on her forehead as she sat at the head of the table, enjoying her birthday cake and good wishes from her friends. Saint Barbara looked tired.

This fall made me angry. With the installation of the chair alarm, Mom had stopped falling during the day. It only seemed logical to get something similar for nighttime. I was tired of vague references by the Homeplace managers to regulations that prohibited bed alarms or hospital beds. I was determined to read the North Carolina regulations for assisted living facilities myself, and, if necessary, contact the state health department to petition for an exception. Heck, I was going to be in Raleigh in a couple of days. I could go to the offices of the Department of Health and Human Services in person! I was sure I could make a cogent argument that some kind of nighttime restraint was essential to Mom's safety.

When I found the regulations (fairly easily, on the Internet) for Licensing of Homes for the Aged and Infirm, I was furious with myself for waiting so long. The only requirements were a doctor's order for the use of a hospital bed with rails, and patient or legal guardian permission to use this form of restraint. Barbara and I both had Power of Attorney documents, and everyone at Seasons treated us if we were Mom's legal guardians. This was going to be easy.

I emailed a copy of the regulations to Barbara so she could talk to Kathy, the director of Homeplace, and Letty, Head Nurse at Seasons.

Tell them we're going to get the order in a few days, when Mom has her follow-up appointment with Dr. S., I wrote.

Mom rarely used her walker anymore, so Barbara and I wheeled her to and from the car in her wheelchair to transport her to the doctor's office. She hugged me and seemed to be in good spirits, though quiet and somewhat withdrawn. She greeted Dr. S. and answered his questions about her stitched-up forehead.

"Does it hurt?" he asked.

"No."

"Do you remember falling?"

"Not really."

"Remember?" Barbara prodded. "I met you at the ER?"

"Oh, yeah. That was a while ago," Mom said.

"Well, you seem to healing well," said Dr. S.

Mom smiled.

Barbara and I changed the subject to our request for a hospital bed. Barbara explained to both Mom and the doctor that the railings would prevent her getting out of bed on her own—the only way we could see of preventing more falls.

"I think it's a good idea," said Dr. S., as he turned to face Mom. "So, you'll be getting a new bed."

"Alright," Mom said.

As he wrote the order, indicating that the railings were to be used only at night or when Mom napped, I asked quietly what he thought about Mom's being so detached.

"She doesn't seem like herself," I said. "Do you think she's had a little stroke or something?"

"Maybe. But this is just how it is, I think. There's nothing we need to do." he replied.

The truth had a Zen-like simplicity that soothed me.

After the consultation, we all went back to Barbara's house for dinner. I held the kitchen door open while Barbara and Phil each put an arm under one of Mom's arms, and all but carried her up the steps. Once settled in her favorite chair, Mom closed her eyes and napped while Barbara and I put dinner together. I fixed a plate of cheese and crackers and poured some wine for the three of us, diluting Mom's portion about one-to-one with water. We enjoyed our aperitif while watching one of Mom's favorite TV shows—a *M*A*S*H* rerun—with the sound turned up so she could hear. The days of our witty banter over cocktails were over, but it still felt homey and companionable.

Just after 7:00 P.M., Mom said she was tired and ready to go back home. I loved hearing her refer to Seasons that way. I took her back on my own, and helped her get ready for bed. While she brushed her teeth with the new electric toothbrush that made it much easier for her, I noticed the box of Depends sitting on the back of the toilet—but Mom had been wearing her usual nylon panties under her clothes. I decided to ask her.

"Mom, do you usually wear these Depends?"

"Only at night," she said, as if it were the most natural thing in the world.

I helped her use the toilet, then slipped on the padded underwear.

As I tucked her in, I reminded her about the hospital bed that would come in a few days.

"Tell me about it tomorrow," she yawned.

I hugged her.

"I'm so glad you're here," she said.

"Me, too."

The next morning, Barbara and I took a short walk around her neighborhood. Ice had formed on some small puddles, and I had to borrow one of her fleece jackets to keep warm. I decided I would stay in with Mom and maybe watch a movie. I hoped the next day would be warmer, so Barbara and I could take Mom out for lunch. I wanted to pamper her, to make up for all the time I wasn't around.

On the way to Seasons, Barbara and I stopped at the medical supply store and ordered Mom's hospital bed, which would be delivered the next day. Because we had the doctor's order, Medicare would pay part of the rental cost. I picked up some sandwiches for Mom and me, then Barbara dropped me off at Seasons for a nice, long visit.

Mom and I enjoyed a picnic in her room. I chattered about Klein, work, friends of mine she knew but barely remembered, and vacations Klein and I might—or might not—take in the coming year. She listened, nodded, and occasionally asked how long I was staying in New Bern. We looked at pictures from her birthday party. I asked her about her cut, but she had forgotten about it.

After lunch, I found an old movie on television, but had no idea what it was. Within minutes, we were both dozing. After a brief nap, I wandered down to the dining room and made myself some tea. While Mom slept in her chair, I straightened up her drawers and closet, pulling out several items that had food stains. I figured I'd help Barbara by doing some laundry. It was getting harder to keep Mom looking neat and tidy, but I was sure it made her feel better. I know it made me feel better.

Dena arrived at around 3:30, and we visited and joked about her being Mom's third daughter. When Mom woke up, Dena made her some tea, and we all talked. Well, Dena talked—entertaining us both with tales of her travels to see other clients, and mishaps at the grocery store. I laughed, sometimes feeling truly amused. Mom smiled but remained quiet, as if hanging out at the edge of the party. After an hour or so, I called Barbara to pick me up.

It always felt so strange to leave Mom "alone." Of course, she wasn't alone. Dena was there, and Mom would be going in for dinner soon—but part of me thought we should all be together—me, Barbara, and Mom—when we were in the same town, the way it had been at her condo in New Port Richey. I knew she was in the best possible situation for her at this point in her life. Maybe I just didn't want that to be so.

"Mom," I said, "Barbara and I will come get you for lunch tomorrow, if the weather is good. Okay?"

"I'd like that," Mom said.

I wrote a note about the lunch plan on the white board hanging next to Mom's closet, hugged Mom and Dena, and left.

Mom loved going to lunch at Sweet Tomatoes. She'd first been to one of the restaurants in the 1980s, when she had visited her brother in California. She'd even written to the company, telling them they should open one near Tampa—and when they did, she took credit for having given them the idea! New Bern didn't have a Sweet Tomatoes, but there was a new place that featured a similar menu of soup and sandwiches with a salad bar. Mom loved it. She and I had lentil soup,

Barbara chose the gumbo, and we all shared a turkey club sandwich. Mom spilled a little soup on her sweater, but then again, so did I.

As we wheeled Mom into her room at Seasons, the first thing we saw was the hospital bed, and it looked awful—all the bars were up, and the mattress was covered with a thin plastic-lined cotton cover.

"Where's my bed?" Mom cried.

"This is your new bed," I said, trying not to sound as freaked out as I felt. "Remember, Dr. S. wanted you to have a hospital bed."

"That's not true. No one told me about this," she moaned.

I noticed Mom's sheets and bedspread hung across the back of her chair.

"Here, Barbara and I will make up the bed with your sheets. Let's see how it looks."

Barbara helped Mom to the bathroom and then into her chair while I got busy making the bed. Mom propped her forehead on her hand, crying quietly.

"Everything is changing," she said. "I don't know what's going on."

Barbara finished up the bed while I hugged Mom and agreed with her.

"I know it's hard," I said. "Nobody likes change. But I think this will be a good change. I really think you'll be more comfortable."

Mom blew her nose.

"Well, that's something that doesn't change," I said, imitating her loud nasal honk.

We all laughed, even Mom.

"And look at your bed now," I said.

Barbara had lowered the railings, added the bedspread, and folded Mom's handmade afghan across the foot of the mattress.

"It does look better," Mom said, wiping her eyes and nose. "I'll try it."

We never heard another word from Mom about the bed. We did hear from the staff; they loved it. Mom never again tried to get out of bed by herself, probably because it was impossible with the railing up. She rang the bell, and an aide came to help. Barbara had made her last midnight run to the emergency room.

Throughout the rest of January and February, Mom continued to decline mentally and physically. I suspected a series of small strokes, called transient ischemic attacks (TIAs), in which clots or tears in small vessels cut off blood flow to parts of the brain. Twice, Barbara found her sitting in urine-soaked slacks, even after reminding the staff to take Mom to the bathroom regularly and dress her in Depends all the time.

"She keeps telling them to get her regular underwear," Barbara told me.

"Just take away her nylon panties," I suggested. "Replace them with Depends. Then the aides can honestly tell her that's all there is in the drawer."

It worked. Between the Depends and a regular toileting schedule, Mom stayed mostly dry.

I found it almost impossible to talk to Mom on the phone. She had grown too weak to hold the receiver up to her ear, and her speech grew slow and garbled. I started sending her short notes and cards every other day. Dena called me from Mom's room twice a week, holding the receiver to Mom's ear.

"How you doing Mom?" I asked.

"Pretty goo' for ole lish." Even with her slurred speech, I recognized her upbeat answer—*Pretty good for an old lady.*

"Are you getting my cards?"

"I li' fun culsh," she answered, letting me know she still preferred telephone calls. Despite feeling reprimanded, I liked that Mom was still opinionated.

She didn't know what day it was or what was happening in the outside world, but she didn't care. She was happy. With a little coaxing, she'd participate in almost anything. She played catch in the common room as the recreation staff tossed around a small rubber ball. She attended bingo. Dena pushed her in the wheelchair pancake race.

One Sunday, Barbara went to visit Mom, and ended up staying two hours.

She had one of her "I hate being old" meltdowns, Barbara wrote in an email. *She cried for about half an hour. I just let her cry it out, and wiped her face with a damp towel. It seemed like a good catharsis for her, though I needed a stiff drink when I got home.*

There were more good days than bad, and when it was warm, either Barbara or Dena would take Mom outside on the Seasons porch.

Mom sat with eyes closed, her face turned to the sun. She looked positively blissful, Barbara wrote in an email.

Mom seemed to be living in the present, moment to moment. I wanted that for her. Heck, I wanted that for me.

Barbara joined Mom for the Seasons celebration of St. Patrick's Day 2010, complete with green balloons, tablecloths, and green cake with green icing. In a photo from that day, Mom exudes *Erin go Bragh* (Ireland forever)—a cheerful leprechaun in a tacky green plastic bowler. Her back is straight, her head is up, and she's smiling her beautiful smile right into the camera. *Mom forever!*

In just two weeks, we would be calling in hospice care.

Mom on St. Patrick's Day, March 17, 2010.
Photo taken by Homeplace staff.

Chapter 22

About a week after St. Patrick's Day, Mom's decline steepened. While her spirits stayed high, everything else drooped. Barbara kept me apprised of the changes.

"Mom lists toward the left, and her left arm (the one on her mastectomy side, the side she fell on last August) can't support her. We prop her up with pillows." Barbara's description on March 20th painted a vivid and sad picture.

"Should I come up?" I asked.

"No, I don't think so," she replied.

"Is she eating?"

"Yes, but someone feeds her, because she has trouble holding a fork. I do it, if I'm there at mealtime."

Two days later, on March 22nd, Barbara told me it had become almost impossible to understand anything Mom said.

"I know," I said. "I called her yesterday. I asked how she was, told her I loved her, and assumed she said 'I love you, too.' I didn't really understand anything, but I got a brief update from Dena."

"I hate to keep asking her to repeat herself," Barbara groaned. "Sometimes I can figure out what she wants, but not always."

"Must be frustrating," I said.

"For both of us."

"It sounds like her muscles are weakening everywhere, or maybe she's having little strokes, or both. Maybe I should come up." I wanted some kind of sign.

"No, I don't think so. You're coming next month. That should be fine."

My routine quarterly visit to Mom was planned for April 14th to 18th, 2010, sandwiched between my friend Bill's yearly visit to our home in Florida and the annual Management and Leadership Conference for the National Hospice and Palliative Care Organization.

"Mom is starting to have trouble swallowing," Barbara told me a few days later. "They are going to purée her food." I heard forced calm in her voice, like she was trying not to frighten me. It frightened me a lot.

"Barb, this does not sound good. I think I need to come up earlier than planned."

"I don't know what to tell you. I don't want to make things sound worse than they are. But then again, I don't want you to be surprised when you get here."

With help from the Seasons caregivers, Mom was still getting dressed every day and going to the dining room for meals. She was always delighted to see Barbara and Dena. Once, she asked Barbara how long she was staying in New Bern, making it seem like Mom thought Barbara was me. Barbara joked that I shouldn't worry about being away, as I was there in spirit. I wondered whether Mom had corrected herself after the fact, but I didn't ask. If she really was beginning to confuse Barbara with me, I didn't want to know.

On Friday, March 26th, Barbara told me that Letty, the Seasons head nurse, had suggested we consider hospice care for Mom.

"So, she's letting us know that Mom is getting near the end, right?" I asked.

"She said we have some time to think about it," Barbara replied. "But yes, we can all see the change in Mom."

Things had been so uncertain for so long—and the uncertainty had been so unnerving—that it was a relief to have Letty give us some clear direction. I was also relieved to be moving into an area in which I felt competent. I knew what to do when it was time for hospice care, and knowing what to do, I got busy.

"I've done a lot of work with The Carolinas Center for Hospice and End of Life Care. I'll call to see what info they have about hospices in New Bern."

It was too late to call The Carolinas Center that Friday, so I checked their website and emailed the names of two hospices to Barbara. She talked to Letty, who identified one of the two as the hospice Seasons typically worked with.

If they have experience with one of them, I'd go with it, I wrote in my email reply. *Everything will be easier if the two agencies have a good working relationship. I suggest calling them sooner rather than later. The hospice nurse will do a thorough assessment, and it could really help us understand what's going on. If they don't think Mom needs hospice care, they won't put her on their service. If hospice is right for her, then the longer she has it, the more she'll benefit.*

On Monday, I talked with colleagues at The Carolinas Center. The executive director reminded me that they couldn't really recommend one hospice over another. Then she told me, off the record and as a friend, that she felt either of the two I had named would be a good choice.

Barbara emailed me after her visit with Mom on Tuesday, March 30th.

I'm going to call the hospice tomorrow, she wrote. *Mom's no worse than she was last week, but she's no better, either.*

After she called the hospice, she called me.

"I talked to Alice, the hospice administrator," Barbara told me. "She said they have a long and excellent relationship with Homeplace and Seasons. The nurse will come tomorrow to do the assessment, and I'll be there."

"Good," I said. "I'm looking Alice up on their website. I like that she's an RN."

"I told her all about you, and that you would be part of all decisions. I also let her know you would be calling her."

"Good. Good. I'll want to talk with the nurse after the assessment, too," I said. "Maybe you can get her to call me before she leaves."

"I'm sorry this is happening so fast, but I think it has to."

I was up and pacing around my office. I stopped and leaned over the desk to pet the cat on the windowsill. She tucked her head, rubbing her ear on my hand.

"No, it's good. It's hard, but it's good. I'll wait to talk to the nurse, but I'm pretty sure I'm going to come up—not wait until the 14th." I hoped the nurse would be able to give me a better sense of Mom's condition, and, though I hated the thought, how long she might live.

"Whatever you want," Barbara said. "I don't know that it's urgent, but, well, I just don't know…period."

It was nearly 5 P.M., and I felt too keyed up to call Alice. I'd call her in the morning.

It had been exactly two weeks since Mom's happy leprechaun photo.

I waited until 9:30 the next morning to call Alice at the hospice office. I knew how busy mornings could be, as the overnight on-call staff updated the day staff and everybody figured out their schedule of home visits.

When Alice came on the line, I introduced myself as Barbara's sister, and reminded her that Mom was scheduled for an assessment that afternoon. She had been expecting my call. I told her about my hospice background. I wanted to talk with her, hospice professional to hospice professional.

"I know there won't be a care plan for Mom until after the assessment, but I wanted to make sure everyone knows we understand what's happening, and that we're on board with the hospice approach to care," I said.

I felt my throat catch as my attempt at detachment failed miserably.

"I'll bet this is hard for you," said Alice.

Her compassion shattered my reserve. I reached for a tissue. All that knowledge and experience had prepared my brain to know what was happening, but nothing had prepared my heart for the crushing loss.

"Yes. I know what kinds of hard decisions are coming. But we're lucky. We know that Mom doesn't want any extraordinary measures—no tube feeding, nothing like that," I said. "She's told us she's ready to go."

"Well, let's see what Tammy, the nurse, finds later today," said Alice.

"Yes, and then please have her call me. I'm trying to decide when to come up to North Carolina."

"I'll do that. And feel free to call me anytime."

I hung up, and then let myself cry it out. As her daughter and as Mom's friend, I was grateful for the hospice professional inside me, but she wasn't in charge any more.

I managed to work in short spurts throughout the day, and even conducted a conference call with a client. Someone mentioned it was April Fool's Day. I thought about sending Barbara an email. *Maybe Mom is fooling us,* it would say. As I started to write, it didn't seem clever anymore. I made a quick trip to the grocery store, and forgot the chicken I wanted for dinner. My thoughts were on what was happening in New Bern, and on when I should get on a plane. I checked flight options on the Internet.

Alice called me at around 5:30 P.M. They expected to enroll Mom in hospice care the next day, based upon Tammy's assessment. Barbara had signed the Notice of Election, a form to tell Medicare that Mom wanted to "elect" the hospice benefit. Medicare pays for hospice care if the patient agrees to give up their regular hospital benefits (meaning no more visits to the hospital, which was fine with us) and accept non-curative, palliative care only. The other requirement was that two doctors, one of whom could be the hospice physician, must certify that the patient has six months or less to live if their illness follows the expected course. We knew Dr. S. would sign the form, and that Mom would be admitted the next day.

"Her diagnosis is Alzheimer's dementia," Alice told me.

"What? Really?" I was quiet as I quickly ran through some hospice regulations in my mind. "I'm surprised," I said, "but I understand you have to have something—something that meets the required guidelines."

When a person becomes a hospice patient, the hospice must identify the "terminal diagnosis," and they need documentation from the patient's medical record that supports that diagnosis in order to meet Medicare regulations and receive payments. For someone like Mom, who didn't have any of the usual diseases that cause death—cancer, heart failure, lung disease, liver or kidney failure—but who did have memory issues and difficulty swallowing, the diagnosis they could best support was "Alzheimer's and related dementias."

I didn't see Mom as an end-stage dementia patient. She still knew us and communicated her thoughts and desires, even though she had trouble speaking. For me, she was still Mom deep inside, just old and wearing out, body and mind.

If it had been up to me, Mom's terminal diagnosis would have been "failure to thrive," a term typically applied to infants, or "debility, unspecified." (Both of these official diagnoses are found in the *International Classification of Diseases* [ICD-9], a standardized diagnostic tool maintained by the World Health Organization and used by healthcare providers and payers across the United States.) But neither of these diagnoses fit Medicare criteria for hospice.

Alice shared more information from Mom's assessment, and filled me in on the initial care plan. Tammy would be the primary nurse, and would visit three times a week. A nursing assistant would be assigned to help with personal care, and would coordinate her visits with Seasons. Alice told me Mom would also be visited by the social worker and the chaplain, who would decide after their assessments about additional visits.

"Mom will tell the chaplain she's an atheist," I warned Alice. "I don't understand her views, but I accept them."

"Well, Annie, our chaplain, will be available all the same," she said.

"What about her prognosis?" I asked.

"Well, we never know, of course. She seems fairly stable right now," Alice replied.

Something about the way she said "stable" conjured a mental picture of Mom balanced on the edge of the bed—perfectly still, but in danger of falling. Now I was sure; I had to go to New Bern and see for myself just how stable—or not—she was.

I called my friend Bill to talk about his planned trip to Miami.

"I have to go up," I told him. "But you could come down anyway, and get some sun. My mother might be fine, and then I could come back in a couple of days and still spend the weekend with you. But I won't know until I get there."

"Look, I'd rather postpone until you're around. I've got tons of work, anyway," Bill said. "I'm just so sorry this is happening."

I called Barbara and told her I would be coming up on Tuesday.

"I'll fly into Raleigh-Durham and drive down. I should be there by 4:00 P.M."

"Mom and I will both be glad to see you," Barbara said. "Also, I sent a memo to Homeplace with the information about Mom's contract with the National Cremation Society."

"Okay, but don't you think you'll be there? Can't they call you if something happens?"

"I guess. I don't know. I was thinking that the call would have to come from a healthcare provider."

"Yeah, that makes sense. Anyway, it's good to make sure everyone has the info—that we're all on the same page."

"One weird thing," Barbara continued. "Mom's been really thirsty, asking for water all the time—but she has trouble swallowing it, and kind of chokes and coughs."

"I'll check with my hospice doc buddies. Maybe they've seen this before."

"Tammy, the hospice nurse, is going to bring some thickener that we can put into any liquid. Apparently, that makes it go down the right way and eliminates choking."

"Never heard of it, but I trust the hospice. Still, I'm going to email Ira."

Dr. Ira Byock, a longtime colleague, and I wrote the *Missoula-VITAS Quality of Life Index* together. He has published several books on end-of-life care, and remains one of the best hospice docs ever. As I typed an email to him, I described Mom—failing in all activities of daily living (ADLs), unable to stand alone even while holding a grab bar, eyes closed most of the time (though not sleeping), and often seeming to drift. Then I sat back in my chair, shocked at the truthfulness of the image I'd conjured.

I asked about Mom's thirst. Had he seen this before? Did he have any suggestions?

Ira wrote back within the hour. He said Mom might be "dry," meaning, I suppose, dehydrated. He recommended a simple work-up with blood tests, if she seemed uncomfortable. Barbara said Mom did not seem uncomfortable, just thirsty, and with the thickener, she was able to swallow better. She had even enjoyed a cup of coffee for the first time in days.

Barbara and I agreed to avoid any kind of testing unless it would change the plan for her care or medications. We decided to tell everyone to give her as much as she wanted to drink.

The day before my trip, Barbara sent an email.

I just talked to Dena about her afternoon with Mom, she wrote. *Despite the yellow pine pollen that is now the scourge of New Bern, she and Mom spent a good part of the time outside. Mom drank two big glasses of thickened water over the course of an hour or so. Dena says she talked to Mom a lot (no surprise), and Mom tried to talk back, but Dena could only understand about a third of what she said. At least once, she told Dena she was happy at Seasons, and Dena said she smiled a few times. All in all, an encouraging report, I think.*

The next morning, Tuesday, April 6th, Klein drove me to Miami International Airport. I didn't want to park my car in the airport garage, as had been my custom. I wasn't sure how long I would be gone.

Chapter 23

I DIDN'T STOP ONCE ON THE DRIVE from Raleigh-Durham airport to New Bern. I was surprised how quickly I ticked off my usual checkpoints—Smithfield, Goldsboro, Kinston. One minute I thought I might be too late, and that Barbara would call and tell me Mom had died. The next, I thought Mom would be fine, and I'd be heading back home in a day or so.

As many times as I'd been to New Bern, I always got confused about which way to turn at the top of the exit ramp. This time, I turned right—the correct way for Barbara's house—without a thought.

Barbara met me in the driveway with a big hug.

"How are you doing?" she asked.

"I'm fine. I just want to see Mom."

"All right, let's put your suitcase in the house and go right over. Do you need a snack or anything?"

"No, let's go."

As we drove to Homeplace, Barbara told me that the hospice had started Mom on a low dose of Lortab, a form of codeine, for overall comfort.

"Mom's heart rate was elevated this morning. Tammy, the hospice nurse, said she might be in some kind of distress, but Mom denied any pain, even though Tammy asked the question all different ways."

"Did you see her after she took it? It's an opioid, a narcotic, so it can make her sleepy until she gets used to it."

"I don't know if they've started it yet. Tammy said they were prescribing a low dose, but on a regular schedule, and they'll adjust it to keep her comfortable but awake. And honestly, she's often kind of drowsy anyway. She's really changed since you last saw her."

"I know. Don't worry. I get it."

And then we were there, in Mom's room. She looked up from her wheelchair perch and smiled at me. I wrapped her in a big hug.

"I'm so glad to see you," I whispered to her.

"Me too," she whispered back, though it came out as "misha."

Mom was in bad shape, but I was neither surprised nor alarmed. Barbara had prepared me well. Mom's left arm was swollen and useless. Her left fingers were permanently bent inward to meet her palm. Her right arm and hand trembled with any effort, and calmed only when held or resting on the arm of her chair. Mom's eyes searched my face, and while she looked somewhat confused, there was no doubt she knew me and was happy to see me. I was filled with a melting tenderness for Mom, and for Barbara.

It turned out Mom hadn't been whispering to me. As she tried to say something else, I realized her speech was nearly inaudible, and she could barely form words. With difficulty, we understood her to ask if we were going to Barbara's house for dinner, as was customary when I visited. I looked at Barbara, silently asking if such a thing was even possible.

"We were thinking we'd do that tomorrow night," Barbara said to Mom. "But we'll stay and keep you company here while you have dinner."

As if on cue, one of the nursing aides came to get her for the evening meal. Everyone acted as if Mom was still her old self, though clearly she was not. She didn't complain or seem distressed, so I joined in. She was still among the living; we would treat her as such.

We wheeled Mom to the dining room, and talked with others at the table until Mom's plate of pureed food arrived. She accepted a few bites of a spinach and egg mixture that I offered on a spoon. She ate without any apparent interest or enjoyment.

"Are you hungry, Mom?" I asked.

She made a sound that I recognized as "No."

"Alright," I said. "I won't force you."

Letty heard me, and she came over to encourage Mom to eat a little more. Mom said something I couldn't understand.

"She wants something to drink," Barbara interpreted for us.

Letty got her some thickened juice. Mom finished all of it, and then we went back to her room, where she asked for water.

Barbara and I sat with her for a while, offering her water and chattering to fill the silence. I talked about my work, my friends, and a book I was reading. After a while, we took Mom to the living room where she always spent her evenings, telling her we'd be back in the morning.

On the way out of Homeplace, I asked Barbara if she had the makings for a Manhattan at her house.

"Bought it all yesterday," she replied, without looking at me.

That was Tuesday.

At 8:00 the next morning, Barbara and I stopped in to see Kathy, the Homeplace/Seasons Director.

"How is your Mom doing?" she asked.

"She's very weak," Barbara said, "but we're hoping to take her to my house tonight for my famous beef stew."

"Is the hospice working out?" Kathy asked.

"They've been great," Barbara answered.

"Kathy," I said, "Can she stay here, even if she gets worse? I mean, is it okay? Can she die here?" I wiped away a tear. "I want her to be in her own place."

"It's fine," Kathy said, passing me a box of tissues. "This is her home."

Barbara and I found Mom in her room. She was dressed and propped up in her chair. I had planned on a quick "hello" before going to the gym, but as we hugged Mom and sat down, Tammy, the hospice nurse, arrived. She checked Mom's blood pressure, pulse, and respirations, and asked her if she had any pain.

Mom said, "Muh," which meant "no."

"Mom, can you see all right?" I asked. "Your glasses looked smudged."

I took her glasses, breathed on them moistly, and then wiped them with my t-shirt. I put them back on her face.

Mom smiled and said, "Let there be light!" clearly enough. We all laughed, and I gave Barbara a knowing look. *See*, my eyes said. *She's still in there.*

"This might make you kind of sleepy," Tammy said to Mom as she gave her the 9:00 A.M. dose of liquid Lortab.

"I'll stay with her," I said. "I can go to the gym later."

Barbara and I had brought two cars so we could go our separate ways. She returned home to cover a work call.

As Mom drifted off to sleep in her chair, she called out softly, "Help, help."

"Mom, are you alright?"

She nodded.

"Did you know you were calling out for help?"

"Muh," she mumbled.

I hugged her gently as she slept. I thought about all the times she'd lain down with me at night in my tiny twin bed to help me fall asleep. I felt sad, and inexplicably calm.

When Mom woke up about twenty minutes later, she wanted water. I thickened it as Barbara had taught me, and she drank it through a straw. Then she wanted to go to the bathroom. I didn't trust myself to help her now that she was so weak, so I found the nurse's aide.

As the aide wheeled her out of the bathroom, Mom said she wanted to lie down. She curled up on top of the bedspread, and I covered her with the crewel-work afghan she'd made twenty-some years earlier. It was decorated with fanciful mushrooms and vines, and edged with hand-crocheted fringe.

"You did such beautiful needlework Mom," I said.

"I love you," she murmured, as clearly as she could. Her words caressed me like a soft spring breeze.

"I love you, too, Mom."

Once she fell asleep, I decided to run errands and go to the gym. I pulled up the bed rail and let the staff know she was napping. I told them I'd return in a few hours. Dena was due to arrive at noon.

I drove to UPS and dropped off a package of tax documents for Mom's accountant. As far as he knew, she had just signed her Form1040. I stopped at Target to buy more Pull-ups for Mom, spent forty-five minutes pounding on the elliptical trainer at the gym, and went to the house for a snack. While there, I composed an email to Bill, my friend who had postponed his Florida visit.

Mom seems generally in good spirits, I wrote, *and very accepting of help. Yesterday, she said she "feels old," and "It's hard to be old." She is getting great care, and I'm so glad I am here to just be with her. I don't know when the end will come, but we are all as ready as we can be. It may be months, but not many. Tonight, we will bring her to Barbara's house for dinner.*

A short four hours later, my message would have been very different.

I headed back to Mom's at around 1:00 P.M., planning to drop off the Pull-ups, have a brief visit with Dena, and then go back home for a shower. Mom was up in her chair, and after hellos and hugs and *I love yous*, she drank some water.

"She asked me to call both you and Barbara," Dena said.

Mom looked at me and I saw confusion, or maybe fear, in her eyes.

"Mom," I said. "What's wrong? Are you hurting?"

She made the sound that meant "no." Then she gestured for more water.

Dena made conversation, asking if I had been to the gym, though it was obvious from my workout clothes and stringy hair.

"Yes, I know I need a shower. Probably smells like a good idea," I joked. "Right, Mom?" I chose to see a little smile on her face.

When an aide came and took Mom to the bathroom, Dena grabbed my hand.

"She told me she's dying," Dena said.

"Well, I think maybe she is," I said. "What do you think?"

"Sometimes she seems good, but not today. She's always in my prayers."

Mom lay down under the afghan again. She continued to ask for Barbara, so I called the house and told Barbara what Dena had said. When Barbara arrived, Mom woke up.

"I'm here," Barbara said.

"Good," Mom said, then asked for water.

After giving Mom a drink, Barbara asked her, "Is everything okay?"

"Okay," she said, closing her eyes.

Dena, Barbara, and I sat together, watching Mom sleep, listening to her breathing and chatting quietly. I sat next to the bed, occasionally stroking Mom's arm if she whimpered.

After an hour, Barbara and I encouraged Dena to go home, assuring her we'd stay until Mom woke up.

"You call if you need me," Dena said as she blew a kiss to Mom. We nodded.

Mom slept fitfully for another couple of hours, her regular breathing punctuated by frequent, very soft cries of "Help, help." She woke every twenty minutes or so wanting water. Barbara read poems to her in a soothing sing-song while I stroked her back and legs.

"Everything will be alright," I whispered, hoping it was true.

"There's no way we can take her to dinner," I said to Barbara. "I'll go to the house to shower, and come right back. Then you can go home, finish up the stew, and bring some back for Mom."

"Sounds good. I'll tell the nurses that Mom won't be going to the dining room tonight."

As soon as I walked through the locked door out of Seasons, I started to cry. Ducking into the restroom, I locked the door and yanked out a handful of paper towels. I buried my face in the stiff folds, letting myself wail. My life with Mom was ending. She was moving on without me. I knew it was time, and I knew we would both be fine. I swam in a pure, clear lake of sadness—no islands of regret or weedy tangles of anger, no longing to alter the course. After a few minutes, I took a deep breath, washed my face, and walked to the car.

When I got back to Seasons, Mom was sitting up in bed, wearing her nightgown.

"Melly will stay here while I go home and get the beef stew, okay?" Barbara asked Mom. "We'll all have dinner here in your room."

"Shoo," Mom said, which we took to mean "sure."

I turned on the television and watched the news. I pulled the chair up next to the bed and held Mom's hand. She seemed more awake, though her eyes were often closed. Each time I offered her water, she drank some.

Barbara was back within half an hour, bringing the stew, bowls, and spoons. She'd prepared a special portion for Mom, chopped fine and thickened with tiny pieces of bread. Mom lit up when Barbara came in presenting the picnic, but when I offered her a spoonful of stew, she took the smallest bit on her tongue, chewed a bit and then let it fall from her mouth.

"Do you want something else, Mom?" I asked.

"Wal," she said, her sound for "water."

"Maybe you'll be hungry tomorrow," I said, as I reached for her water glass and straw.

After one more trip to the bathroom, the aide tucked Mom into bed. Barbara and I hugged her and she fell asleep. We stayed for an hour or so, nibbling on room-temperature stew. Mom slept quietly without waking or calling out.

"Do you think we should stay all night?" I asked Barbara.

"She seems pretty peaceful right now," Barbara answered. "Maybe we should go home and get some sleep. We may need to start staying with her soon."

We told the night nurse to call if there was any change, or if Mom asked for us. Barbara and I both slept with phones by our beds.

That was Wednesday.

Chapter 24

THE NEXT MORNING, I walked through the door to Seasons at 7:30 A.M. Mom wasn't in her room. *Maybe she's feeling better,* I thought. I hoped.

Sure enough, I found her up and dressed in the dining room. But she wasn't at her usual table. She sat in her wheelchair, by herself, away from the other residents. Instead of a plate of breakfast, a glass filled with about two ounces of pink liquid rested on the table beside her.

I greeted her with a smile and leaned in for a hug. As she lifted pale blue eyes to meet mine, I saw something unfamiliar—sadness, or perhaps alarm.

"How are you feeling?" I asked her.

She mumbled a reply that I understood as, "Not so good."

As I hugged her, she was, for a moment, completely intelligible. "I think I'm dying."

"Oh, Mom!" I hugged her tighter. "I think so, too. But don't worry. Barbara and I are here, and everything is going to be okay."

The truth had slipped out naturally, riding on a wave of extraordinary calm. Later I would wonder if all my hospice experience had led to this one moment.

"I think I'll take Mom back to her room," I said to the nurse, who was administering medications to the residents at other tables. "She's not feeling well."

"Well, she needs to have that medicine to relieve any pain she might be feeling." The nurse pointed to the pink liquid, Mom's Lortab.

I promised to help her drink it all.

"I'll come with you," said the nurse. "We thought she might perk up if we brought her to the dining room, but I guess not."

The nurse sat with us for nearly ten minutes, gently lifting the glass of pink liquid to Mom's lips again and again. *Where do they find these people?* I wondered, and thanked God for bringing us to Seasons.

After the nurse left, Mom dozed in her chair.

"Help." Each exhale carried the whispered cry, the very sound of her breath.

I wondered what she was feeling and seeing behind closed eyes.

I tried to console her with hugs, soothing words, and gentle rocking. I gave her water whenever she woke and asked for it.

Later in the morning, Barbara relieved me so I could be on a conference call that I should have cancelled. I was back in the room by 11:00 A.M. Mom was napping on the bed, covered by her afghan. No need to use the side rails any longer. We wouldn't be leaving her alone.

"Tammy, the hospice nurse, was here while you were gone," Barbara told me. "She said Mom showed nonverbal signs of pain, or at least discomfort, and she got an order for a low dose of morphine."

"Instead of the Lortab, right?" I asked.

"Yes. I guess she thinks the morphine will work better. And she left these."

Barbara picked up a bag of little pink sponges, each stuck on a cardboard stick like a lollipop. I recognized them—mouth swabs to keep Mom's mouth moist, if and when she stopped drinking. We were already smoothing ChapStick onto her dry, flaking lips.

I sent Barbara home to get some lunch, and a few minutes after she left, Mom woke up. I carefully took her to the bathroom, noting how much weaker she was, and then got her settled in her armchair.

"Dena will be coming in a little while," I told Mom, taking her hand.

Just as I turned on the television, Tammy walked in.

"I'm back," she sang. "And I brought you a milkshake."

I almost laughed out loud. Now I was on the receiving end of the hospice milkshake legend. When I had been in training for my first hospice job, we were told about hospice founders who would go out at 3:00 A.M. to fulfill a patient's request for a milkshake. The only appropriate question, we were taught, was "What flavor?" Mom hadn't asked for a milkshake, but Tammy knew Mom hadn't eaten, and hoped she'd accept the frozen treat.

Tammy offered Mom a spoonful. Mom shook her head, and then reluctantly sipped from the spoon.

"Mom, do you want some more?" I asked.

"Muh," she answered.

"That means no," I translated for Tammy.

"Try another spoonful," Tammy cajoled.

Mom again accepted it reluctantly and swallowed.

"No more," Mom said. And though it was garbled, both Tammy and I heard her clearly.

"Thanks anyway," I said to Tammy.

"It's okay," Tammy said. "Just make sure she gets the morphine every hour. It will keep her comfortable, but it's important that she gets it regularly."

Dena came at 12:30, bringing her usual breath of fresh air. We were all relying on Mom's third daughter to help keep our spirits up. I left the two of them alone, and took a break to eat something and take care of a few emails.

By mid-afternoon, Barbara and I were back in Mom's room. Mom had laid down again, fully dressed, to take a nap. She slept on and off. She was restless, as if being tugged between this life and the next. More than once, Mom had said she was ready to go, but some part of her seemed to want to stay.

"Please help," she breathed, or sometimes, "Please, God, help."

No atheists in foxholes, I thought.

Barbara and I took turns rocking her and reading to her—sometimes from *The No. 1 Ladies' Detective Agency*, which I had pulled off her shelf to pass the time and calm my thoughts, or *Now We Are Six*, children's poems by A.A. Milne that Mom had read to us.

"We love you, Mom. We're here to help you," I whispered. "Everything will be all right. You can let go."

Every hour, we got the Seasons staff to give her the prescribed morphine, and asked for reassurance that Mom was not in pain. I had learned in my hospice training that involuntary vocalizations were normal at this stage of dying, but needed to hear it all again. Training was abstract. This was real.

Mom was still asking for water. We would either crank up the head of the bed and give her some thickened water using the straw, or, more and more often, we offered one of the pink sponges soaked in water. She sucked them greedily, and we rewet them two, three, four times.

Around 4:00 P.M., Barbara walked Dena out to her car. Mom was curled up facing the wall. I was hugging her, almost laying in the bed with her. She opened her eyes and looked up at the pastel-colored photo of Barbara and me as children.

"Beautiful girls," she murmured.

"Love you, Mom," I whispered, my eyes hot.

Over the next hour, Mom seemed to grow more agitated, waking more often and drawing her legs up to her abdomen. She looked as if she were hurting.

"I don't think the morphine's working," I said to Barbara at around 5:00 P.M.

Barbara talked to Letty. It turned out a higher morphine dose had been ordered. I called the pharmacy to find out when the medicine would be delivered, and found out they had not received the prescription. I was frantic. I got the hospice on-call nurse on the phone.

"My mother seems pretty uncomfortable. She's supposed to get a higher dose of morphine, but the pharmacy doesn't have the prescription," I explained.

"Don't worry," she said. "I'll check into it and call you right back."

Fifteen minutes later, she called to tell me the prescription had been faxed to the pharmacy, and the morphine would be delivered by 6:00 P.M. If a mistake had been made, they'd recovered quickly. I felt relieved. No wonder all the research I had done as a consultant for hospices showed such high satisfaction ratings!

Even after the higher morphine dose at 6:00, Mom was still restless, more frequently moaning or calling for help. Barbara called the hospice and asked to have the nurse visit. I offered Mom some water. She refused, but sucked hungrily on one of the wet sponges.

Thirty minutes later, Leona, the on-call nurse, arrived. Where Tammy was lithe and perky, Leona was comfortably rounded and calming.

"I think your Mom is going through what we call a 'transition,'" Leona explained. "We'll keep giving her a little additional morphine until she is comfortable."

Then Tammy arrived, and the two nurses worked together to gently get Mom into her nightgown, making sure she was clean and dry. Still, almost an hour after Leona had arrived, Mom was not settling down.

"We're going to give her a little Ativan," Leona said. "It's for anxiety."

"I know it well," Barbara said. "I take it myself when I need it."

Tammy broke the pill in half and placed one piece on each side of Mom's tongue, where it would dissolve slowly. Over the next twenty minutes, Mom settled and fell asleep. It was 8:00 P.M.

Barbara and I decided we would take turns staying overnight.

"I'll stay tonight." I knew I wouldn't be able to sleep anywhere else.

"Okay. I'll bring you some dinner. What do you want?" Barbara got up to leave.

"Just a sandwich, and maybe a cookie."

Around 9:00 P.M., Barbara dropped off a paper bag filled with goodies from her kitchen, along with a pillow and blanket. She blew a kiss to Mom so as not to disturb her, and hugged me.

"I'm so glad you're here," she said.

"Me, too."

I spread out my picnic on Mom's small round coffee table—a ham sandwich with mayonnaise and lettuce on Pepperidge Farm white bread, potato chips, sliced apple, and several cookies. It was just like the lunches Mom had packed for us in elementary school—with one difference. Instead of a carton of milk, Barbara had included a Manhattan in a mason jar, with a separate baggie of ice. After an appetizer of tears and Kleenex in the bathroom, I sat down to supper.

Mom slept quietly as I ate, read my book, and then turned out the light to doze a bit. At 11:00 P.M., an aide came in to check on her, and before I could intervene, she woke Mom to see if she needed a dry Pull-up. I couldn't help being angry.

"You have no idea what it took to get her to sleep," I said, and then apologized. "It's not your fault. You didn't know. But she's not doing very well."

"I'm so sorry," she said. And, though we had never met, she hugged me.

Mom was now awake, so I offered a wet sponge. She took only the tip into her mouth. As I used the sponge to moisten her lips and tongue, I noticed that half of the Ativan was still undissolved. I spread the now-mushy tablet along her tongue so it would be absorbed, then sat close to the bed, holding her hand and stroking her arm until she fell asleep again.

I pulled Mom's two armchairs close together with the seats facing, to make a very short bed. I got as comfortable as I could with the pillow and blanket, and after a while, I fell asleep.

That was Thursday.

I was already half out of my chair-bed at around 2:00 A.M. to check on her when I realized Mom was awake. I moistened her lips and mouth, but she didn't suck on the pink sponge. Mom had stopped eating two days earlier. Now she was finished with drinking.

I got the Seasons staff to give her a dose of morphine and she slept again, but fitfully. She'd half-wake—continuing, though less frequently, to moan or call for help, and draw up her knees. It seemed as if she was working hard at something. I could almost imagine her swimming across a river or crossing a burning desert, from life to death. I wanted to pick her up and carry her to safety. I told her I loved her. I rocked her, and said that Barbara and I would be all right without her.

Mom had another dose of morphine at 4:00 A.M., but she never seemed to relax. Did she need more Ativan? At 5:30, I called the hospice and asked to speak with the on-call nurse. Leona called me back, and I took the phone into the bathroom so as not to disturb Mom.

"Can you come?" I pleaded. "Her breathing seems louder and raspier. But even if she doesn't need you, I think I do." I was too exhausted to cry.

"I just need to get dressed," she said. "Give me thirty minutes,"

Barbara arrived before 6:00 A.M. with coffee in hand. Leona came in a few minutes later.

"She's refusing even the mouth swabs," I told them.

Leona listened to Mom's chest. She checked to make sure Mom was dry, and let us know that Mom probably would not make any more urine, especially as she had stopped drinking.

"Her breathing is a little more liquid, but still sounds pretty good," she said. "I'll give her the next dose of morphine, and Tammy will come by later."

When Mom fell asleep, Barbara sent me home to get some rest.

Back at the house, I fixed myself an egg and toast, and felt better after I ate. I tried to work on some email, but nothing made sense. I took a short nap and a long shower. Phil called from work to say he would bring home Chinese take-out for dinner. I named him "Number-One Assistant" to Saint Barbara.

When I got back to Seasons, Mom was still sleeping. Barbara and I stayed with her throughout the morning, each of us slipping out now and then to take a break.

Around noon, Dena arrived, and Barbara went out to get lunch for the three of us. We chatted quietly, nibbling at our bagel sandwiches until Mom woke up. She had slept more than six hours, which was good, but now she seemed to be in pain, which was bad. We should have awakened her to give her morphine, but as she had been sleeping so quietly, we assumed she was comfortable. Still, I knew better from my years in hospice work. Round-the-clock medicines must be taken as prescribed to keep the blood level up. Daughter Melanie needed to channel Dr. Melanie more often.

Fifteen minutes or so after a dose of morphine and an Ativan on her tongue, Mom calmed down and slept quietly off and on the rest of the day. Letty was on duty at Seasons, and managed to give Mom the morphine regularly without even waking her.

Dena left at 3:30. I walked her to the car and gave her a big hug. The next day, Saturday, was her day off.

"Be sure to call me if anything happens," she said.

"You know I will."

Barbara and I sat by Mom's bed, reading or watching her sleep.

"If you could just give her the pill, wouldn't you do it?" Barbara asked me.

I thought about it. Wasn't that what I had meant when I'd said I wanted to carry Mom to safety? Hadn't I wanted to end it for her, quickly and painlessly? I closed my eyes.

No, I thought, *I wouldn't*. Whatever was happening felt unexpectedly natural to me, even sacred—something to behold without judgment or interference.

"I suppose so," I lied.

Barbara wasn't wrong to want to spare Mom any further, pointless suffering. I'd always thought myself capable of "pulling the plug," but at that moment, I was relieved that the decision was not in my hands.

Tammy showed up at 5:30 P.M. She checked Mom's blood pressure and pulse, straightened the sheets, and gently changed Mom's position, but only slightly.

"Make sure she gets the morphine every hour, even if she is sleeping. She will need it now. We don't want her to suffer," Tammy told us. "I'm on call tonight, so I'll come back at 9:30 to see how she is doing."

Barbara and I took turns going to the house to have some dinner. Barbara changed into comfy clothes, and gathered up her toothbrush and pillow to spend the night.

At 9:30, we reconvened with Tammy. Mom was sleeping. We were keeping her lips moist with the swabs and ChapStick. She had not spoken all day. Her breathing was shallow and raspy, but regular.

"I think she could use a little more Ativan, but her prescription has run out, and I'm not sure how soon we can get some more," Tammy told us.

"Do you want an Ativan?" Barbara asked.

"Do you have one?" Tammy asked.

"I do," said Barbara, pulling a pillbox out of her purse.

"Are you okay with this?" I asked Tammy.

"I am if you are," she replied.

"We are," Barbara and I said, looking at each other.

Tammy checked the dose and said it would be best to give it to Mom rectally, as she had so little saliva. Barbara and I stepped out to give Mom privacy. Then Tammy called us back into the room. We helped her settle Mom into a more comfortable position.

"I don't think she needs any more morphine. I think she will pass easily now, on her own," Tammy said. "I think it will be sometime tonight, or tomorrow."

That was Friday.

After Tammy left, Barbara and I talked quietly.

"I don't want to go to the house," I said.

"But you're exhausted," Barbara said.

"I am, but I know I won't sleep."

"At least go stretch out on the couch in the parlor," Barbara said.

I took the pillow Barbara had brought the night before, and Mom's afghan. The parlor was at the front of the Homeplace building. The furniture was comfortable, and the room smelled disinfectant-clean. Light spilled in from the main corridor, but the couch was in a darkened corner. I closed my eyes, not expecting to sleep, then jerked awake as the door chime bonged, and bonged again. I watched the day shift leave, and the night shift arrive. One of them asked me if I was all right.

Then I slept again, until I felt a hand on my shoulder, gently waking me. Barbara sat on the coffee table, looking at me.

"It's over," she said. "It was quiet. She just stopped breathing."

Silent, I bundled up the afghan and pillow as we both stood and walked toward the hallway. I touched Barbara's arm and pulled her into a hug.

My watch said 1:45 A.M.

It was Saturday, April 10, 2010.

Chapter 25

THE LOGISTICS WERE SIMPLE. Barbara called the hospice, and Tammy came over right away. The Seasons night nurse called the funeral home—the one Barbara had identified, the one that would honor Mom's longstanding contract with the National Cremation Society.

It turns out that funeral homes have a man available in the middle of the night to carry away your loved one. He will arrive as if he has just stepped from behind a desk, dressed in a suit and tie, shoes shined. He will not look tired. He will not say much, but his few words will reach you on palpable waves of compassion. Perhaps, like me, you will wonder how he can seem to care so much about one more person, one more body, at 2:30 in the morning. Maybe he is simply adept at reflecting grief.

We were home by 3:00 A.M. Barbara poured herself a shot of Maker's Mark, and I sipped some red wine. We collapsed on the sofa in the family room.

"It's so weird," I said.

"I know," Barbara replied.

"I mean, she's gone, but where did she go?"

"It makes me wish I believed in the kind of heaven where she could be reunited with Daddy, and with her mother. It makes me wish she believed in it."

"I guess I don't think she's anywhere, but maybe everywhere—like a little bit in you, and in me, and in everyone she's known and touched in some way."

We sipped our drinks. I leaned my head against the back of the couch and closed my eyes.

"I don't know if I'll sleep, but I need to lie down," I said.

Barbara slid over and hugged me.

"Sleep as long as you can. We'll figure everything out tomorrow," she said.

We took the rest of Saturday off. We slept late. After I called Klein, Phil drove us to Beaufort just to get away from New Bern. We had lunch by the harbor, then wandered the docks. Barbara called Dena. I called mom's best friend Lenore, who agreed to let Ginny know, and Susan, the manager of Gulf Harbors in New Port Richey. I remember bright, hot sunshine, and feeling dull and gray by comparison. My eyes hurt.

It took only a day and a half to clean out Mom's room. Some of her clothes went into bags for Goodwill, some we threw away, and some we left for the Seasons staff. I packed up all the family heirlooms from the étagère for transport to Barbara's house, where we would divide them up. After clearing it with Letty, we decided to leave most of the furniture, which she would offer to the staff.

Dena joined us on Monday morning. We gave her Mom's garnet ring and matching earrings, and one of the bird figurines·from the étagère. We told her she was welcome to take any of the furniture she wanted. We let her give us one dollar, so if anyone asked, we could say she had paid for the items.

"What are you doing with that?" Dena pointed to the portrait of Barbara and me as children in our poufy dresses.

"Well, neither of us wants it," I said, "so I guess we'll just get rid of it."

"Could I take it?" Dena asked.

Barbara and I looked at each other.

"Uh, sure," Barbara stammered.

"I think it's pretty, and it will remind me of you two every time I see it," Dena said.

We helped her load the two-foot-square picture and a small table into her car, then hugged her and said our goodbyes.

"I'm gonna write you," Dena called.

"I'll write back," I said.

"What in the world are her friends going to think when they see that portrait hanging in Dena's house?" Barbara chuckled as we walked in from the parking lot.

"Gotta love her!" I said.

On Monday afternoon, Barbara and I met with the funeral director. We declined to have Mom's cremains made into pendants or dolphin statues. Mom had not left instructions about where to scatter her ashes, but she had scattered Daddy around their New Port Richey condo. I thought she might like to join him there. Barbara and I agreed to have Mom's cremains shipped to me so I could take her "home."

Mom's estate had been in the best possible shape when she died. All of her assets were in either the joint bank account she had shared with Barbara, or the revocable trust that named Barbara and me as successor trustees. That meant we could cover all her bills by writing checks, and then distribute the remaining funds when we were ready. Even so, it would be several months before we worked out all the details of how to close the trust and file taxes for 2010.

Mom's will contained instructions for certain bequests to friends—Lenore, Ginny, and Susan—and she had left handwritten notecards for each of them. Though there was no obligation to make these bequests (the trust took precedence over the will), Barbara and I knew why Mom had named these people in her will. She wanted them to celebrate their treasured friendships with her. Before I left New Bern, we wrote the checks and sent the cards with our cover note.

Several days after my return to Miami, I stopped at my neighbor-hood Starbucks and ordered a cappuccino to go. While I waited for the barista to make the drink, my friend Kim called to see how I was doing.

"I'm at Starbucks, 95th Street," I said.

"I'll walk the dog over and meet you." Kim lived just six blocks away.

I found a comfortable chair in the corner, and sat down to wait. I never go to the coffee shop without something to do. Usually, I have my computer and a work project. I like to get out of the house, and I find it easier to concentrate when surrounded by quiet conversa-tions that don't concern me. Sometimes, I bring a book. That day, I had nothing to occupy my mind while Kim gathered up the dog and walked those six blocks.

I rummaged in my purse for something to read. I found a grocery list, a bunch of receipts from the Harris Teeter in New Bern, and a copy of Mom's living will. More than a year earlier, I had reviewed the legal document, then put it in my purse. I'd carried it with me all that time without ever looking at it—two pages bearing the letter-head for the Law Offices of H. Curtis Skipper, P.A., New Port Richey, Florida. The memo was addressed in all capital letters:

TO MY FAMILY, MY PHYSICIAN, MY ATTORNEY, MY
CLERGYMAN:
TO ANY MEDICAL FACILITY IN WHOSE CARE I
HAPPEN TO BE:
TO ANY INDIVIDUAL WHO MAY BECOME RESPONSIBE
FOR MY HEALTH, WELFARE, OR FINANICAL AFFAIRS.

The first page included a declaration—*Death is as much a real-ity as birth, growth, maturity, and old age*—and her wishes for the end of her life: her desire to avoid the *indignities of deterioration, dependence, and hopeless pain*; her desire that her death not be arti-ficially prolonged, and that she be permitted to die naturally, with

medications to provide comfort; her wish not to have artificial nutri-
tion or hydration; her acceptance of the consequences of refusing
medical treatment when it was determined she was terminally ill;
her hope that those who cared for her would feel legally and morally
bound to fulfill her stated wishes; and her intention, through the
living will, to relieve us from making these difficult decisions, and to
place that responsibility on herself.

"I just don't want to be a burden." She had said it so many
times, in so many ways. This document laid out the strength of her
convictions.

Reading that living will, I was flooded with relief. We had honored her wishes. We had found compassionate caregivers who had
spared Mom from being completely dependent on us—perhaps her
biggest fear. We had let her go naturally, without tubes or machines.
I wondered, *is this why I came to hospice work? To prepare me for this
death?*

Still, as sure as I was that Mom had died on her own terms, there
were aspects of the final years of her life that I'll never be sure about.
Did we wait too long to move her to North Carolina? If we had forced
her into assisted living, or to have a caregiver at night, could we have
prevented the big fall that precipitated her decline—or would those
changes have dampened her spirit, which could have been as devas-
tating as the fall? Did the pacemaker surgery, meant to improve her
quality of life, actually diminish it by landing her in rehab?

I had been haunted by these decisions at the time they were made.
I thought writing about it all would dispel the ghosts. Instead, I have
come to think that doubt is the nature of this beast. We can never
be certain what constitutes the "best" option when caring for aging
parents. We can only try to discern what seems right at the moment.
Barbara and I always erred on the side of preserving Mom's independence, knowing how fiercely she claimed it. Had that been best for
her? It was never easy for us.

What puzzles me most is why, over and over again, Mom chose
Barbara. She chose to move to New Bern, not Miami. She chose to
die when she was alone with Barbara. And, on the second page of her

advance directive, she designated Barbara as her primary healthcare surrogate, with me as back-up if Barbara was "unwilling or unable."

The language was legalese—boilerplate. Mom never doubted whether she could count on Barbara. And Barbara, who perhaps never thought she would be chosen, who never expected to be "the one," who was perhaps more able than willing, had stepped up in every way. When I overreacted out of emotion, Barbara could be more dispassionate, and therefore more effective.

I'll never know whether Mom thought it through, whether she had a plan. I do know, however, how it turned out. She spared me the enormous burden of her day-to-day care—a job I would have taken on without question, and with such fervor that I would have risked my job, my health, and my marriage. Mom and I had been close for years; we were *sympatico*. She did what she thought was best for me. She protected me.

At the same time, she forced her way into Barbara's life at a point when Barbara couldn't say no. For her part, Barbara not only accepted the mantle thrust upon her, she excelled in the role of caregiver. She did laundry, went along on outings with the "geezers," entertained Mom at home, and baked her birthday cakes. She became "the good daughter" that Mom had always wanted her to be, and they both knew it.

Barbara also took care of me. She eased me into Mom's decline, always seeing it more clearly than I did, but never forcing me to accept more than I was ready for. She was gentle with Mom and with me—forcefully, purposefully gentle. In assuming the brunt of Mom's care, Barbara gave me the space to separate, so I could bear Mom's death.

What Mom spared Barbara was the burden of remorse. I cannot know how Barbara would have felt if she and Mom had remained semi-estranged, because they didn't.

So, what of my vow to make Mom's life the best it could possibly be in the years after Daddy died? The task proved humbling. I had written academic papers on quality of life at the end of life, but as Mom declined, I could only guess at what "quality of life" meant for her. When she told us she didn't need (meaning she didn't want) a caregiver at night, did she mean she valued taking care of herself, by herself, more than she valued her own safety? Was she capable of understanding that distinction? Parenting an adult is not like parenting a child. Even when Mom seemed childlike, she retained the right to autonomy that children have not yet earned.

There exist no training classes for adult children caring for aging parents, and none for our overly independent parents to learn how to accept our care. Barbara and I did as well as we knew how to do, and so did Mom. Even our successes were often painful.

What sustained us after Mom moved to New Bern was a combination of devotion and duty—or maybe devotion *to* duty, even as those duties changed. During Mom's final years, our roles in the Pratt Family Circus slowly altered. Mom went from consummate ringmaster to scary tightrope walker who couldn't remember to wear a safety belt. I stepped back from my place as star performer and tried to adapt to a supporting role, punctuated by the occasional swing on the trapeze. And Barbara went from spectator to the most important role of all—the one who held the net.

BODYFLOW
By Barbara Pratt

After the tai chi moves,
After the sun salutation and Pilates core work
Comes the last part where the instructor speaks soothing words
and the music switches from the wordless ambient swirl to The
Beatles.
When I find myself in time of trouble, Mother Mary comes to me,
speaking words of wisdom, let it be.

And her head floats into mine – why now?

My mother's name was Mary, but that's not what she was called
And this is not a time of trouble, in fact –
The trouble she caused me is now gone, and her own troubles too,
whatever they were.

I wondered so often how her death would come, and especially when,
how soon, how much longer,
And how will it feel, will there be pain?
How will it end? How will it feel? And when?
And how much of that questioning was about her, and how much
about me?

When she came to live nearby at age 91, I couldn't keep my distance
anymore
At first I thought the burden would crush us both
I resented the new anxieties she added to the ones I had been culti-
vating all my life in the garden she helped me plant long ago.
She came to live nearby and her fears and needs came to live in my
head alongside my own.
I often felt there wasn't room.

My actions were exemplary, I flatter myself that she never noticed any flaw in the feelings behind them.

Her smile always showed the purest delight in seeing me, especially as she became less and less sure when she had seen me last.

I longed to feel that same delight, unsullied by any thoughts less worthy.

These days I pass the home where she died almost every day, and I often catch a glimpse of that smile.

The feelings it evoked have not yet distilled down to any pure essence.

But now, lying here on the mat, her other face floats before me, the one I gazed at that night and tried so hard to pay attention to, so that I would know and recognize the answer to my questions.

This is how it ends? This is how it feels?

And I still don't know the words, only the pictures.

MAY 2012

Suggested Resources

Aging Life Care Experts: Professionals who can assess needs, facilitate difficult conversations, help connect families with local resources, and more. The website for the Aging Life Care Association (http://www.aginglifecare.org) offers a search function to locate a professional by zip code, city, and state.

Area Agencies on Aging: Established under the Older Americans Act in 1973 to respond to the needs of Americans sixty and over in every local community. By providing a range of options that allow older adults to choose the home or community-based services and living arrangements that suit them best, these agencies help older adults to "age in place." On the National Association of Area Agencies on Aging website (http://www.n4a.org), you can enter your zip code to find information on any local Area Agency on Aging.

National Alliance for Caregiving: A non-profit coalition of national organizations dedicated to improving quality of life for families and their care recipients through research, innovation, and advocacy. Visit the organization's website (http://www.caregiving.org) to read and download resources for caregivers.

COMPARE websites, provided by the Centers for Medicare and Medicaid Services (CMS): Websites facilitating comparison of the quality of specific healthcare providers in your area. Medicare COMPARE websites exist for nursing homes, hospitals, physicians, home health services, and dialysis facilities; new COMPARE sites are added periodically (Hospice Compare is scheduled for release in 2018). Search for the site you want—for example, "Nursing Home Compare" or "Dialysis Facility Compare."

National Hospice & Palliative Care Organization (http://www. nhpco.org/about/hospice-care) and State Hospice Organizations: Trade organizations for providers of hospice and palliative care. Contact them by phone, or use their websites to find information about hospice services and providers of hospice and palliative care in your community.

Village to Village Network: A national organization committed to helping members age in the place of their choosing with close connections to their community and with the supports they need. Visit the website (www.vtvnetwork.org) to search for a "virtual village" in your area, and to learn how the network supports local villages.

The Conversation Project: A grassroots public campaign spanning both traditional and new media to make it easier for people to talk about their wishes for end-of-life care. The Conversation Project team includes five seasoned law, journalism, and media professionals who are working *pro bono* alongside professional staff from The Institute for Healthcare Improvement. Visit their website (http:// theconversationproject.org) for information, easy-to-use guides, and other resources.

***Holding the Net* website:** I created this website (www.holdingthenet. com) to offer additional information and resources, including material submitted by readers.

Suggested Additional Reading

Byock, Ira, M.D. *The Four Things That Matter Most—10th Anniversary Edition: A Book About Living.* New York: Atria Books, 2014.

Casey, Nell. *An Uncertain Inheritance: Writers on Caring for Family.* New York: Harper Perennial, 2007.

Gross, Jane. *A Bittersweet Season: Caring for Our Aging Parents—and Ourselves.* New York: Knopf, 2011.

Hodgman, George. *Bettyville, A Memoir.* New York: Penguin Books, 2015.

Morris, Virginia. *How to Care for Aging Parents.* New York: Workman Publishing Company, Inc., 2014.

Pipher, Mary, Ph.D. *Another Country: Navigating the Emotional Terrain of Our Elders.* New York: Riverhead Books, 1999.

Sheehy, Gail. *Passages in Caregiving: Turning Chaos into Confidence.* New York: HarperCollins Publishers, 2010.

Acknowledgments

WRITING IS SOLITARY WORK, but making a book is not. Two wonderful groups of writers contributed their time and talent to every chapter of *Holding the Net*. For invaluable feedback on the manuscript, I thank the members of my Miami writing group—Andrea Askowitz, Betsy Blankenbaker, Nicholas Garnett, Jeff Weinstock, Maureen Daniel Fura, Jeanne Panoff, Vanessa Michel Rojas, and especially Christina Freedman, whose belief in the project was a constant touchstone for me; and my writing group on Cape Cod—Hugh Blair-Smith, Tamsen George, Sandy Macfarland, and especially Barbara Sillery, who not only read multiple drafts of each chapter, but also shared publishing advice. I also thank the following talented authors whose workshops and classes helped shape my writing: Ann Hood, Les Standiford, Jacquelyn Mitchard, Dani Shapiro, and Joyce Maynard. I am indebted to Cathi Hanauer, who provided skillful editorial contributions and generously shared her expertise as my manuscript developed into this book. Thanks also to family and friends (my beta readers), who provided comments and suggestions along the way—especially Lea Roark, Kate Callahan, Irma Emery, my husband Klein, and, of course, my sister Barbara—and to Cathryn Lykes for skillful copyediting and proofreading. To my "retreaters"— Karen Steinhauser, Gwynn Sullivan, and Jeanne Twohig—thank you for fanning the embers of my desire to write until I could no longer ignore the conflagration. And to my dear friend Mary Porter, thank you for introducing me to Dede Cummings of Green Writers Press/ Green Place Books.